SPECLANG
Beiträge zur Berufs- und Fachkommunikation

Band 5

Herausgegeben von
Beata Grzeszczakowska-Pawlikowska, Jacek Makowski
und Agnieszka Stawikowska-Marcinkowska

Die Bände dieser Reihe sind peer-reviewed.

Joanna Kic-Drgas / Violeta Jurkovič

Paths of Purpose

A Journey into LSP Teacher Development

With 21 figures

V&R unipress

Bibliografische Information der Deutschen Nationalbibliothek
Die Deutsche Nationalbibliothek verzeichnet diese Publikation in der Deutschen
Nationalbibliografie; detaillierte bibliografische Daten sind im Internet über
https://dnb.de abrufbar.

Die Veröffentlichung wurde von der Abteilung für Sprache und Literatur der
Adam-Mickiewicz-Universität Poznań, der Fakultät für moderne Fremdsprachen und dem
Institut für Linguistik der Adam-Mickiewicz-Universität Poznań mitfinanziert.

Gutachterinnen: Prof. Dr. Yasemin Kirkgöz (University of Çukurova, Türkiye),
Dr. Olinka Breka (University of Zagreb, Croatia)

© 2024 Brill | V&R unipress, Robert-Bosch-Breite 10, D-37079 Göttingen, ein Imprint der Brill-Gruppe
(Koninklijke Brill NV, Leiden, Niederlande; Brill USA Inc., Boston MA, USA; Brill Asia Pte Ltd,
Singapore; Brill Deutschland GmbH, Paderborn, Deutschland; Brill Österreich GmbH, Wien,
Österreich)
Koninklijke Brill NV umfasst die Imprints Brill, Brill Nijhoff, Brill Schöningh, Brill Fink, Brill mentis,
Brill Wageningen Academic, Vandenhoeck & Ruprecht, Böhlau und V&R unipress.
Alle Rechte vorbehalten. Das Werk und seine Teile sind urheberrechtlich geschützt.
Jede Verwertung in anderen als den gesetzlich zugelassenen Fällen bedarf der vorherigen
schriftlichen Einwilligung des Verlages.

Umschlagabbildung: © Violeta Jurkovič
Druck und Bindung: CPI books GmbH, Birkstraße 10, D-25917 Leck
Printed in the EU.

Vandenhoeck & Ruprecht Verlage | www.vandenhoeck-ruprecht-verlage.com

ISSN 2750-6169
ISBN 978-3-8471-1690-5

Contents

Preface 9

1. Context 13
   1.1. Introduction 13
   1.2. Poland 14
      1.2.1. Presentation 14
      1.2.2. Educational system 15
      1.2.3. Language policy 20
      1.2.4. LSP teachers – legal regulations 21
      1.2.5. Status of LSP teachers 23
      1.2.6. LSP provision in higher education 24
      1.2.7. Subjects supporting LSP teacher education at universities . . 26
      1.2.8. LSP teacher education 26
      1.2.9. LSP conferences, associations and journals 29
   1.3. Slovenia 30
      1.3.1. Presentation 30
      1.3.2. Educational system 31
      1.3.3. Language policy 35
      1.3.4. LSP teachers – legal regulations 36
      1.3.5. Status of LSP teachers 38
      1.3.6. LSP provision in higher education 39
      1.3.7. Subjects supporting LSP teacher education at universities . . 41
      1.3.8. LSP teacher education 41
      1.3.9. LSP conferences, associations and journals 42
   1.4. Synthesis 43

2. Introduction to LSP 47
   2.1. Introduction 47
   2.2. Definition 47
   2.3. Needs analysis in LSP 51

2.4. LSP curriculum and syllabus design	55
2.5. LSP materials design	60
2.6. LSP teaching methodology	63
2.7. LSP assessment	65
2.8. Synthesis	68
3. LSP teachers	**71**
3.1. Introduction	71
3.2. LSP teacher roles	72
3.3. LSP teacher competences	74
3.4. LSP teachers' knowledge of the discipline and knowledge of language use in context	77
3.5. LSP teacher identity	80
3.6. LSP teacher challenges	84
3.7. LSP communities of practice	86
3.8. Synthesis	88
4. LSP teacher professional development projects	**91**
4.1. Introduction	91
4.2. TRAILs	91
4.3. Catapult	96
4.4. LSP-TEOC.PRO	98
4.5. Synthesis	103
5. LSP teacher education and professional development	**105**
5.1. Introduction	105
5.2. Literature review	106
5.3. Methodology	113
5.3.1. Research questions	113
5.3.2. Instruments and data collection	114
5.3.3. Data analysis	115
5.4. Results	116
5.4.1. Similarities and differences in the pre-service education of LGP and LSP teachers	116
5.4.2. Elements of disciplinary knowledge essential for LSP teachers	120
5.4.3. Development of disciplinary knowledge of LSP teachers	122
5.4.4. Similarities and differences in the continuous professional development of LGP and LSP teachers	124

  5.4.5. Role of collaboration in the education and professional
    development of LSP teachers 126
 5.5. Synthesis 129

Conclusion 133

List of tables 137

List of figures 139

References 141

Preface

This publication is, and should be seen as an invitation, an invitation to travel and discover the still untrodden paths of the education and professional development of teachers of languages for specific purposes (LSP). For several reasons, we hope that this publication is unique. Firstly, the subject of the pre-service education and in-service professional development of LSP teachers is still a poorly researched topic, if only because of the great diversity and dynamic changes occurring in the professional sector. Secondly, it offers a non-perspective view of the topic, a theoretical review of the literature, practical solutions proposed within the framework of implementation projects (two of which the authors participated in as leaders of Polish and Slovene teams), and the authors' empirical research, presenting the opinions of language teacher educators in the context of pre-service education and in-service professional development of LSP teachers. Thirdly, the innovative dimension of this publication lies in the comparison of two similar but nevertheless different educational contexts – Polish and Slovene – in which the LSP teacher is confronted with constant challenges.

The aim of this publication is to point out the main aspects of LSP teaching (such as needs analysis, curriculum and syllabus design, materials design, or assessment), while highlighting the role of LSP teachers, their competences and career paths. These considerations will form the basis for the formulation of the possibilities for the pre-service education and in-service professional development of LSP teachers based on qualitative data collected in Poland and Slovenia among language teacher educators.

This publication consists of five main chapters, a preface, and conclusions. It opens with this Preface, which includes the main aims and objectives of the book, and the characteristics of the target audience of this publication. The first chapter is a description of the context of LSP teaching in Poland and Slovenia. It provides information on the educational system in both countries, the language policy in place, the legal regulations concerning the profession of LSP teachers and their legal status. The chapter goes on to point out the paths of LSP teacher education in both countries, the associations that promote new trends in LSP teaching and the networking of teachers through conferences. The second chapter thematises the basic areas of LSP teaching, starting with the definition of LSP, then through needs analysis, the development of syllabuses and curricula, the preparation of LSP teaching materials, the choice of appropriate teaching methodology and, last but not least, assessment. The focus of the next chapter, the third, is placed on LSP teachers. This chapter describes their roles and competences, pre-service and in-service education, and professional development programmes, LSP teacher identity, and the professional challenges they need to negotiate in their teaching contexts and along their careers. The fourth chapter is devoted to EU projects implemented so far in the field of LSP teacher education and professional development in response to the growing and diversifying needs of experienced and future LSP teachers. In this section, three projects – TRAILs, Catapult, and LSP-TEOC.Pro – are presented through their main aims, objectives, and results. The fifth chapter is the result of interviews with language teacher educators in Poland and Slovenia, and is a kind of change of perspective in describing the relevant elements of pre-service education and in-service professional development, which are previously presented on the basis of accumulated literature. The book closes with conclusions with a summary of and authors' takeaways from each main chapter.

    The target group of this publication will primarily be LSP teachers at secondary school or university level, as well as in adult education, since it is hoped that in this publication they will not only find guidance on relevant issues in the field of LSP education and professional development, but will also be able to familiarise themselves with the latest literature and research trends in this field. Also important recipients of the book might be language teacher educators and policy-makers. The latter, in particular, significantly shape the contexts in which LSP teachers need to operate. It is worth mentioning that the book is dedicated not only to experienced LSP teachers, but also to young people who have decided to make this their career. The book can also serve as a signpost for researchers interested in the field of LSP teaching, as well as for those who are planning future research or teaching projects that could shed new light on hitherto undiscovered areas of LSP teacher education and professional development.

    This book does not give a straightforward answer as to what the pre-service education and in-service professional development for LSP teachers should look like instead, its aim is to juxtapose what is certain, or indisputable (theoretical considerations) with what is still in the realm of expectations (the needs of LSP teachers, their concerns, and the challenges ahead). While a lot of research has already been invested in English for Specific Purposes (ESP), other languages are still under researched. In this book we draw a lot of information from available ESP research, but because we are advocates of multilingualism, we will use LSP (and not ESP) throughout. We also hope that this publication will contribute to the development of research into all languages taught for specific purposes and not only English.

We hope that this book will contribute to a better understanding of the situation of the many thousands of LSP teachers in all different corners of the world and, at the same time, intensify efforts to fill the existing but narrowing gap in practical implementations of research findings.

The authors would like to express special thanks to the reviewers: Prof. Yasemin Kirkgöz from the University of Çukurova, Turkey, and Dr. Olinka Breka from the University of Zagreb, Croatia, for their factual and highly constructive reviews. Additionally, we extend our gratitude for the financial support of this publication to Vice-Rector Prof. Dr. Katarzyna Dziubalska-Kołaczyk and the collegial body, The School of Languages and Literatures, Prof. Krzysztof Stroński, Dean of the Faculty of Modern Languages and Literatures, as well as Prof. Danuta Wiśniewska, Director of the Institute of Applied Linguistics at Adam Mickiewicz University.

We wish you an enjoyable and fruitful reading experience.

Poznań, Portorož, 2023

1. Context

1.1. Introduction

Although the use of foreign languages in different professional contexts is becoming increasingly important in the labour market, the preparation of LSP teachers for the challenges of their future professional path, and therefore the provision of various forms of pre-service education and in-service professional development still seems to be a secondary issue. A report prepared by the European Commission (2017) highlights persistent shortcomings in the adequate preparation of LSP teachers for work with different groups of students, which contributes to reduced educational effectiveness in the European Higher Education Area (EHEA) and beyond. Therefore, due to the lack of adequate preparation to teach LSP, achieving the desired outcomes is not always possible (see Kırkgöz & Dikilitaş, 2018).

This is particularly worrying, due to the fact that knowledge of specialised languages not only allows increased professional mobility but also significantly improves the employability of future graduates (see Kic-Drgas, 2022; Kırkgöz & Dikilitaş, 2018), and is therefore an important element of a professional career. However, due to its specificity, resulting from the combination of linguistic knowledge and professional expertise, LSP teaching remains an enormous challenge for pre-service and in-service LSP teachers.

In this chapter, the current situation of LSP teachers will be discussed, with specific focus on their legal status resulting from national regulations, as well the construction of the LSP teacher education curriculum and professional development programmes. The perspectives and challenges of LSP teacher education and professional development will be based on an analysis of the educational landscape in Slovenia and Poland.

The choice of these countries results from the fact that firstly both countries have, in the last decades, undergone reforms of their educational systems that have also influenced the work and professional path of foreign language teachers. Secondly, in both countries LSP teacher education and professional development is developing dynamically, through the organisation of LSP conferences, participation in international projects addressing LSP teacher issues, as well as publications which are a response to the needs of LSP teachers representing different disciplines.

The chapter is divided into two main parts reflecting the LSP teaching context in Poland and Slovenia. First, both countries are presented, then the educational system in each country is described. Next, the definition of the teacher of foreign languages for general purposes (LGP) and LSP teacher in the light of legal regulations is provided. Following that, the status of LSP teachers is highlighted. The next part of this chapter is dedicated to the description of subjects supporting pre-service LSP teacher education at universities, and the presentation of an example LSP teacher education course. Finally, information about LSP conferences, associations, and journals is provided for both countries.

1.2. Poland

1.2.1. Presentation

Poland, with a total area of 312,679 km^2[1], is located in the centre of the Northern European plain[2] and has borders with Germany, the Czech Republic, Slovakia, Ukraine, Belarus, Lithuania, and Russia. Geographically, Poland has access to the Baltic Sea to the north and the Tatra mountains to the south. The capital city of Poland is Warsaw.

The population of Poland is 38.5 million people[3]. It is rather homogeneous, 95% are citizens of Polish origin[4]. However, this situation has recently changed as a result of the war in Ukraine, which contributed to the migration of many Ukrainians to Poland in 2022.

Poland's official language is Polish[5]. This inflectional language is a member of the West Slavic group of Indo-European languages[6]. Polish is spoken as a mother language by some 44 million people worldwide[7].

---

1 http://www.studyinpoland.pl/en/about-poland/14-general-information-about-poland.
2 http://www.studyinpoland.pl/en/about-poland/15-why-poland.
3 http://www.studyinpoland.pl/en/about-poland/14-general-information-about-poland.
4 https://stat.gov.pl/spisy-powszechne/nsp-2021/nsp-2021-wyniki-ostateczne/informacja-o-wy nikach-narodowego-spisu-powszechnego-ludnosci-i-mieszkan-2021-na-poziomie-wojewodz tw-powiatow-i-gmin,1,1.html.
5 https://sip.lex.pl/akty-prawne/dzu-dziennik-ustaw/konstytucja-rzeczypospolitej-polskiej-167 98613/art-27.
6 https://encyklopedia.pwn.pl/haslo/polska-jezyk;4575053.html.
7 https://blog/jakie-sa-gwary-i-jezyki-w-polsce-poznaj-jezyki-urzedowe-dialekty-i-gwary-ziem -polskich/.

In the years 1939–1945, Poland was occupied by the German and Soviet armies. After World War II ended, the nationalisation of the country's economy started, initiated by the Soviets and the Polish Workers' Party. The communists controlled the economy, education, administration, media, and essentially all other domains of Polish life. The Polish party "Solidarność" was formed to protest against the ruling authorities and the intense activities of the party led, in consequence, to the dissolving of the ruling government and the first democratic elections in the country since World War II, which were held in 1989.[8] In 2004, Poland became a member of the European Union.

Poland is a parliamentary democracy with the Polish zloty as official currency. According to Eurostat, the GDP per capita was EUR 13,760 in 2021[9]. The main economic sectors in Poland are wholesale and retail trade, transport, and food industry[10].

In 2020, there were 373 higher education institutions operating in Poland, both public (130) and private universities (243)[11]. Among the 14,800 foreign graduates in the 2020/2021 academic year, the largest number of students are from Ukraine (51.7%), Belarus (8.7%), and India (6.9%)[12].

1.2.2. Educational system

The Polish educational system combines centralised governance (i.e. laws/regulations for which the Ministry of Education and Science is responsible) and decentralised school administrations (for which local authorities are responsible)[13].

The main acts (national and international) regulating the Polish educational system are the Constitution of the Republic of Poland (1997)[14], the Bologna Declaration (1999)[15], and the Regulation of the Minister of National Education of 30 January 2018[16] on the basis of the programme of general education for general

---

8 https://ipn.gov.pl/en/brief-history-of-poland.
9 https://ec.europa.eu/eurostat/databrowser/view/sdg_08_10/default/table.
10 https://efl.pl/pl/biznes-i-ty/artykuly/dominujace-sektory-gospodarki.
11 https://stat.gov.pl/obszary-tematyczne/edukacja/edukacja/szkolnictwo-wyzsze-i-jego-finanse-w-2019-roku,2,16.html.
12 https://stat.gov.pl/files/gfx/portalinformacyjny/pl/defaultaktualnosci/5488/8/7/1/szkolnictwo_wyzsze_w_roku_akademickim_2020-2021.pdf.
13 https://kuratorium.katowice.pl/wp-content/uploads/2022/03/system-edukacji-w-polsce-en.pdf.
14 https://isap.sejm.gov.pl/isap.nsf/DocDetails.xsp?id=wdu19970780483.
15 https://www.ehea.info/media.ehea.info/file/Ministerial_conferences/02/8/1999_Bologna_Declaration_English_553028.pdf.
16 http://www.ilo.org/dyn/natlex/docs/ELECTRONIC/105966/129706/F190023232/D20171632.pdf.

secondary school, technical secondary school, and upper secondary industrial school (Journal of Law 2018, item 467)[17], and the Regulation of the Council of Ministers of 17 December 2020 on the establishment of the Ministry of Education and Science and the abolition of the Ministry of National Education and the Ministry of Science and Higher Education (Grzelak & Roszko-Wójtkowicz, 2017).

The Constitution of the Republic of Poland (1997)[18] introduced free of charge and compulsory education for all citizens until the age of 18. The next important step in the transformation of the Polish educational system was adopting the regulations of the Bologna Declaration (1999) which formulates the fundaments of European higher education respecting diversity of languages and cultures (Eurydice, 2018).

The starting point for the introduction of changes in Polish education was the Regulation of the Minister of National Education of 30 January 2018 on the basis of the programme of general education for general secondary school, technical secondary school, and upper secondary industrial school (Journal of Law 2018, item 467)[19]. The main reforms referred to the structure and division of schools. The regulations introduced compulsory pre-primary education, an 8-year primary school (instead of 6-year and 3-year lower secondary school), a 4-year general secondary school (instead of 3-year upper secondary school), a 5-year technical secondary school (instead of 4-year upper secondary school), master's degree programmes: 1.5 to 2 years, in selected areas: 4.5 to 6 years, third-cycle programmes leading to a doctoral degree: 2 to 4 years. In 2021, two separate ministries, the Ministry of National Education and the Ministry of Science and Higher education merged, and since then, both school and higher education are under the authority of one ministry (based on the Regulation of the Council of Ministers of 17 December 2020 on the establishment of the Ministry of Education and Science and the abolition of the Ministry of National Education and the Ministry of Science and Higher Education (Journal of Laws of 2020, item 2334)[20].

Each level of education is then covered by specific acts, presented in Table 1.

---

17 https://isap.sejm.gov.pl/isap.nsf/DocDetails.xsp?id=WDU20180000467.
18 https://www.sejm.gov.pl/prawo/konst/polski/kon1.htm.
19 https://isap.sejm.gov.pl/isap.nsf/DocDetails.xsp?id=WDU20180000467.
20 https://isap.sejm.gov.pl/isap.nsf/DocDetails.xsp?id=WDU20200002334.

Table 1. Legislative documents that regulate the educational system in Poland

Level of education	Act	Purpose
Pre-school education	Regulation of the Minister of National Education of 23 December 2008 on the core curriculum for pre-school education and general education in particular types of schools. Regulation of the Minister of National Education of 28 February 2019 on the detailed organisation of public schools and public nursery schools.	Preschool education provided by public and private nursery schools.
Basic school	Regulation of the Minister of National Education of 23 December 2008 on the core curriculum for pre-school education and general education in particular types of schools. Regulation of the Minister of National Education of 28 February 2019 on the detailed organisation of public schools and public nursery schools.	Basic education performed by public and private basic schools or as education at home.
Secondary schools, secondary vocational education, upper secondary vocational education, and upper secondary technical education	Regulation of the Minister of National Education of 30 January 2018 on the programme basis of general education for general secondary school, technical secondary school and upper secondary industrial school (Journal of Law 2018, item 467).	Short vocational upper secondary education, upper secondary vocational education, and upper secondary technical education.
Higher education	Regulation on Higher Education and Science (Act 2.0).	Status of higher education institutions and requirements for the provision of higher education activities.

The above mentioned processes indicate that the Polish educational system is still in a transformative state, searching for the most efficient way of adapting to the changes in society (digitalisation, migrations, and interdisciplinarity). Without doubt, the geopolitical situation of Poland, as a country in Eastern Europe and an EU member, also has had a significant influence on the recently introduced changes. Poland joined the EU in 2004, and since then the impact of European educational guidelines can be observed, as for instance the increased significance of teaching foreign languages at almost every level of education, as well as broadening the perspectives of education to include forms of informal education, in line with lifelong learning principles. The current shape of primary education in Poland is presented in Figure 1.

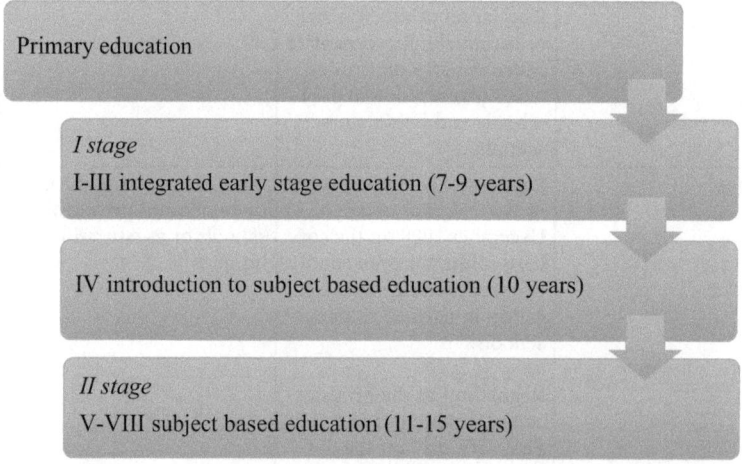

Figure 1. Primary education in Poland (see Grzelak & Roszko-Wójtkowicz, 2017)

Primary education in Poland aims at preparing pupils for their future subject-based education and developing the basic literacy skills, i. e., writing and reading. Compulsory lessons of English as a foreign language start in the first grade (twice a week).

Grzelak and Roszko-Wójtkowicz (2017) name the following key skills that should be developed in primary school: searching, classifying, teamwork and social engagement, solving of problems in various areas, critical analysis of information, mathematical thinking, and active participation in the school, local and broader community. Primary school finishes with an external examination (*egzamin ósmoklasisty*) in Polish, mathematics, and a foreign language (usually English). There are also plans to introduce an additional elective subject, chosen by each pupil, to this exam.

After the completion of primary school, students can choose among the secondary school options presented in Figure 2.

Secondary education aims either at teaching and learning in different fields in general secondary schools (*licea ogólnokształcące*), or the development of

```
┌─────────────────────────────────┐
│ Secondary education             │
└──────────────┬──────────────────┘
               │
               ▼
      ┌──────────────────────────────────────────┐
      │ 4- year general secondary schools (15-19 years) │
      │ or                                       │
      │ 5 -year technical secondary schools (15-20 years) │
      │ or                                       │
      │ 3- year sectoral vocational schools (15-18 years) │
      └──────────────────────────────────────────┘
```

Figure 2. Secondary education in Poland (see Grzelak & Roszko-Wójtkowicz, 2017)

practical skills in technical secondary schools (*technika*), or sectoral vocational schools (*szkoły zawodowe*). Both general secondary schools and technical secondary schools finish with an external examination – the *matura*, which simultaneously represents the entrance examination to higher education studies. At *matura*, mathematics, the Polish language, and a foreign language (usually English) are compulsory, plus students can choose extra subjects in line with their interests and future studies. In technical and vocational schools, students also take vocational school-leaving examinations to check their practical skills (see Grzelak & Roszko-Wójtkowicz, 2017).

Post-secondary education is classified in Poland as part of secondary education. Typically, post-secondary schools provide programmes offering the acquisition of vocational qualifications. The programmes last up to 2.5 years and are aimed at young adults aged 18–20. On the other hand, following the Bologna reform of higher education, higher education programmes are divided into three cycles (Figure 3).

Doctoral programmes usually last 4 years but in exceptional cases by extramural students they can be shortened to two years.

The division of cycles varies depending on the specificity of the field. For example, in science the first cycle can last up to four years and end with the degree title of engineer. There are also examples of long-cycle programmes that last 5 or 6 years and are not divided into separate cycles, such as medicine or law. The number of public schools as well as students attending public schools is higher than non-public. The same tendency can be noticed in higher education[21]. Universities and colleges with teacher education programmes are institutions responsible for preparing future teachers for the teaching profession.

---

21 https://kuratorium.katowice.pl/wp-content/uploads/2022/03/system-edukacji-w-polsce-en.pdf.

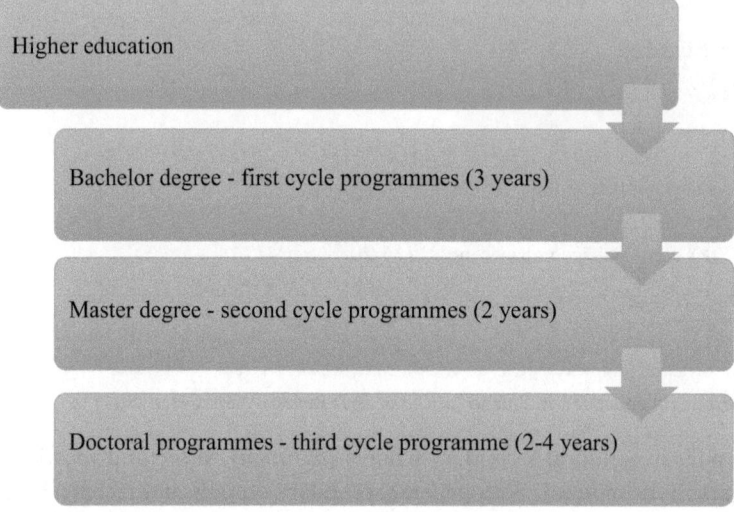

Figure 3. Higher education in Poland (see Grzelak & Roszko-Wójtkowicz, 2017)

1.2.3. Language policy

According to Article 27 of Constitution of the Republic of Poland[22], Polish is the official language in the Republic of Poland. Poland, in comparison with other European countries, is quite homogeneous in both linguistic and cultural terms (Wąsikiewicz-Firlej et al., 2022).

In 2018, approximately four out of 10 Poles declared a lack of knowledge of any foreign language[23]. Among the foreign languages spoken, the most popular is English, with 32% of respondents declaring the ability to communicate in this language, second place is occupied by Russian (20%) and third by German (14%). One in three people in Poland can communicate in at least one foreign language, 10% can speak two, and only three in a hundred speak three foreign languages[24]. According to Centrum Badania Opinii Społecznej (Centre for Public Opinion Research), the command of other foreign languages in Poland was low; few respondents could communicate in French (2%), Spanish (1%) or Italian (0.8%)[25].

---

22 https://www.sejm.gov.pl/prawo/konst/angielski/kon1.htm.
23 https://www.statista.com/statistics/1286134/poland-advanced-knowledge-of-foreign-langua ges/.
24 https://serwisy.gazetaprawna.pl/edukacja/artykuly/1111366,jakie-jezyki-obce-znaja-polacy. html.
25 Centrum Badania Opinii Społecznej (2016). O wyjazdach zagranicznych i znajomości języków obcych. https://www.cbos.pl/SPISKOM.POL/2016/K_005_16.PDF.

Poland's accession to the EU has contributed to an increased focus on foreign language issues. This manifests itself, among other things, in increased funding for the promotion of the Polish language, but also in measures to care for minority languages (Wąsikiewicz-Firlej et al., 2022).

In schools, a compulsory foreign language class (English) starts from the first grade, comprising two sessions of 45 minutes a week. In the seventh grade the first foreign language is taught three times a week for 45 minutes, and a second foreign language is introduced for two 45-minute sessions a week. A foreign language is a compulsory subject in the middle school exam (after the eighth grade) and the *matura* exam[26].

Increasing interest in learning foreign languages has also contributed to the opening of bilingual schools and International Baccalaureate Programmes in Poland.

1.2.4. LSP teachers – legal regulations

The qualifications for teaching foreign languages in public education in Poland were formulated in the Regulation of the Minister of National Education of 1 August 2017[27] on the specific qualifications required for teachers. According to Article 12, which defines the specific qualifications required for teachers, a person who seeks employment as a foreign language teacher needs to have completed:

1. "studies in a second-cycle or long-cycle master's degree in philology with a specialisation in a given foreign language, or in applied linguistics with a specialisation in a given foreign language, and teacher education, or
2. studies in a country where the official language is not Polish, and has a teaching background, or
3. second-cycle studies or a single master's degree, in any field (specialisation), and has
   - a certificate of proficiency or advanced standing in the relevant foreign language as referred to in the annex to the Regulation and teacher education, or
   - a certificate of passing the state examination in the relevant foreign language at level II referred to in the annex to the Regulation, or
4. teacher college of foreign languages in the specialisation of a given foreign language."

---

26 https://eurydice.eacea.ec.europa.eu/national-education-systems/poland/overview.
27 https://www.ilo.org/dyn/natlex/natlex4.detail?p_lang=en&p_isn=105969.

To sum up, the acquisition of qualifications for a foreign language teacher has two main pillars according to Polish law. These are the mastery of the target language and a completion of a teacher education programme. Due to the insufficient number of foreign language teachers in public schools, teachers are allowed to begin working without having completed teacher education but are supposed to complete it as soon as possible (see Kic-Drgas & Woźniak, 2022).

When it comes to nursery schools and the first stage of primary school, a foreign language teacher can be also a person who:
1. has completed studies in the field of teaching, providing preparation for teaching in nursery schools or grades 1 to 3 of primary schools, and an additional teaching specialisation in a foreign language, or
2. has completed a first-cycle programme, a second-cycle programme or an extramural master's programme in teaching, with a specialisation in teaching a foreign language in nursery schools or grades 1 to 3 of primary schools, or
3. is qualified to work in nursery schools or grades I–III of primary schools and additionally holds a certificate of examination in a given foreign language[28].

The second group are university teachers. To teach foreign languages at tertiary level, a background in linguistics and the completion of modern language studies are needed. At tertiary level, there is a division between teaching posts (lecturer and senior lecturer) and research-teaching positions. Teachers in teaching posts give lectures but have no obligation to conduct research, whereas holders of research-teaching positions (full professor, associate professor, assistant professor) are obliged to both teach and conduct research. The position attained as a researcher-teacher is linked to one's academic work and publications. A doctoral degree is not required to teach in tertiary education in Poland. Both groups can teach at all levels of higher education (also the third cycle)[29]. Teaching LSP, however, creates more conceptual problems, as, according to Sowa (2015), the competences that LSP teachers need to have include specialist linguistic knowledge, methodological preparation, and specialist professional knowledge (Figure 4).

Specialist linguistic knowledge means not only fluent knowledge of a foreign language, but also the ability to recognise elements of specific texts and compare them also on contrastive basis (see Kic-Drgas & Woźniak, 2022; Sowa, 2015). Methodological preparation covers not only the planning of LSP classes and presenting material, but also, for instance, adapting teaching strategies to the needs of different target groups. Finally, specialist professional knowledge em-

---

28 https://www.ilo.org/dyn/natlex/natlex4.detail?p_lang=en&p_isn=105969.
29 https://isap.sejm.gov.pl/isap.nsf/download.xsp/WDU20220000574/T/D20220574L.pdf.

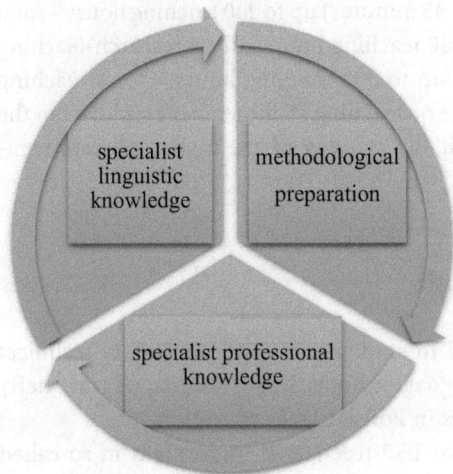

Figure 4. Pillars of teaching languages for specific purposes (Sowa, 2015)

braces the knowledge of the disciplinary content connected with the specific field of LSP taught, for example English for Medicine or Business English.

Although the work of the LSP teacher requires different competences and skills, and also at some points different knowledge, this is not officially regulated through a separate legal act in Poland, which means that becoming a foreign LGP teacher in Poland automatically indicates that the person has been prepared for LSP teaching, too.

1.2.5. Status of LSP teachers

The status of the LSP teacher in Poland is not regulated by law, so there are huge differences between vocational language teachers in secondary schools and those teaching LSP at universities.

The first group mentioned are generally foreign language teachers who, as a result of the reform in 2019, have been forced to teach LSP (Sowa, 2022a). Throughout their career, they start as a trainee teacher, then as an appointed teacher, then a certified mentor teacher. The workload of a teacher in secondary school is 18 hours a week.

The second group are university teachers. To teach foreign languages at tertiary level, a background in linguistics and the completion of modern language studies are needed. Importantly, the position held does not necessarily match the academic title that an LSP teacher holds. Their position affects their status in their institution, their salaries, and weekly workload. "The annual teaching load is (whereby 1 teaching hour is in reality 45 minutes) up to 240 teaching hours – for a research-teaching employee, up to 180 teaching hours – for a research-teaching employee employed as a professor, up to 360 teaching hours – for a teaching employee, up to 540 teaching hours for a teaching staff member employed in the position of lecturer or instructor, if the statutes of the higher education institution provide for such a position"[30].

1.2.6. LSP provision in higher education

In Poland, LSP classes are provided to students in upper secondary technical education, higher education, and language schools. In this section, we will briefly focus on the provision of LSP classes in Polish higher education.

In Polish universities, the need for LSP teachers is transparent in so-called subject universities, namely technical, medical, economic, and so on, where LSP is usually introduced after 2 or 3 semesters of a general English course, and becomes a form of completing the language course. On language degree programmes, LSP features mainly business language, and in rare cases technical or medical language, which are introduced to prepare future translators or teachers, and those classes are focused on terminology more than on communication. LSP provision in philological courses concerns English or German, and in rare cases other languages such as French or Spanish, although also in those cases there is no unified programme. LSP mainly refers to Business English or *Wirtschaftsdeutsch*, again leaving other fields behind. The introduction of the Bologna System, unifying the number of ECTS points in study programmes, also contributed to a reduction in the number of classes which were treated as optional in favour of compulsory courses and a reduction in the number of hours. LSP provision on philology courses is on average 60 hours' maximum in first-cycle programmes but there are also exceptions (see below). For non-philological studies, language learning is provided by a language institute that provides compulsory foreign language courses for the entire university. Generally speaking, foreign language courses may follow this pattern:
– 120 hours for a first-cycle degree programme, lasting for 4 semesters, 30 hours per semester (learning a general foreign language),
– 60 hours in a second-cycle degree programme, taking place over 2 semesters, 30 hours per semester (LSP).

---

30 https://eurydice.eacea.ec.europa.eu/national-education-systems/poland/conditions-service-academic-staff-working-higher-education.

To provide an example, Table 2 presents LSP provision for students of first-cycle and second-cycle degree studies at the Faculty of Modern Languages and Literature at Adam Mickiewicz University.

Table 2. LSP provision for students of first-cycle and second-cycle degree studies at the Faculty of Modern Languages and Literature at Adam Mickiewicz university

	Applied Linguistics (Bachelor degree)		Applied Linguistics (Master degree)	Spanish philology (Master degree)	French philology (Master degree)
LSP course title	Business English Business German	English in Tourism German in Tourism	ESP (Medicine, Business, Law, Engineering)	Spanish for Specific Purposes	French for Specific Purposes
LSP course status	Compulsory	Compulsory	Compulsory	Compulsory	Compulsory
Semester	5/6	5/6	1, 2, 3, 4	2, 3, 4	1
Number of contact hours	60 each language	60 each language	120 h in total (60 h each semester)	30 h (2nd semester) 60 h (3rd semester) 30 h (4th semester)	30 h
ECTS	6 each language	6 each language	16	10	0
Intended course outcomes (example)	Students will be able to use English/German in written in business situations.	Students will be able to prepare a tourist brochure in English/German language.	Students understand and carry out English dialogues, discussions and debates based on knowledge in a chosen field.	Students communicate with specialists in the chosen field in Polish/Spanish.	Students communicate with specialists in the chosen field in Polish/French.

1.2.7. Subjects supporting LSP teacher education at universities

At the outset, it is worth pointing out that an increasing number of language graduates in Poland are finding jobs in business (Gajewska, 2022), as speaking a specialised language can not only be an advantage in finding a well-paid job, but sometimes also a prerequisite for obtaining one. Being aware that the work of an LSP teacher also requires a variety of competences, discussed in detail in a dedicated chapter of this book, resulting from the changing requirements on the labour market, it is necessary to broaden the range of subjects with different knowledge fields offered within the current philology syllabuses in both the first and second cycles. Examples of important subjects supporting LSP teacher education at universities are in particular specialist translation and practical classes on LSP from different disciplines.

Specialist translation is considered one of the key competences in business (Gajewska, 2022) which is why it is valuable also for the future LSP teachers. Since translation is connected to development of the skills that are not directly related to traditional communication in a professional setting, but should be considered more in terms of the proper selection of vocabulary or structures that can be used in specific contexts. Another subject supporting LSP teacher education programmes is an LSP course so that students can experience for themselves the possible difficulties of LSP learners. Different LSP courses are offered in order to prepare future non-philological graduates to work in different fields (business, medicine, law, etc.). However, there is a benefit in those courses also for those who decide to be LSP teachers in future (Gajewska, 2022).

The number of hours and ECTS points dedicated to specialist translation and LSP differs from university to university, ranging from 3 to 6 ECTS points, which shows the discrepancies in the status of these courses. Usually, classes are offered in the form of interactive exercises involving the students. Since the number of hours of LSP courses is usually limited, they cover only very basic topics from the field, and are supposed to be more of an introduction to the topic than an in-depth analysis of complex issues.

1.2.8. LSP teacher education

Pre-service LSP teacher education courses at universities are not very popular, as has been confirmed by research conducted within the Erasmus+ Trails project by Kic-Drgas and Woźniak (2020, 2022a) and John et al. (2023). After investigating 68 institutions in 14 different EHEA countries, only 88 units (full courses, modules) were identified, of which only five were found in Poland. In the following paragraph, the structure and outcomes of one of these courses will be described.

The course's name is "LSP teaching" and it is provided by Adam Mickiewicz University in Poznań, Poland. It is a compulsory course for philology students specialising in foreign language teaching. It encompasses 30 sessions of 45 minutes. It takes place in the fourth semester of the second-cycle degree, and completing this module gives 3 ECTS points. The objectives of the course are to deepen the knowledge and acquire the skills for LSP teaching, to become familiar with ICT use in LSP teaching, and to acquire knowledge about the range of research carried out in the field of LSP teaching.

An obligatory requirement for participation in the course includes graduating from a course in foreign language teaching, seen as general preparation for understanding and dealing with topics connected with foreign language teaching.

After finishing the "LSP teaching" course, the student is able to[31]:
- demonstrate in-depth knowledge and skills in LSP teaching,
- describe the terminology of a given field,
- demonstrate an in-depth knowledge of the field of LSP research,
- use advanced ICT in LSP teaching,
- recognise the need to improve knowledge throughout life, and
- creatively organise the process of teaching others.

The languages of instruction of the course are English and German, since the participants of the course are students of German and English applied linguistics.

The topics covered by the course are presented in Figure 5.

In the course, alongside presentations prepared by the lecturers, active participation in the form of projects (lesson planning and presentation of chosen papers on the subject), discussions, and teamwork sessions (material preparation) is foreseen. Additionally, participants take part in meetings with LSP practitioners in order to learn about the practical aspects of LSP teaching in different fields.

---

31 https://sylabus.amu.edu.pl/pl/1/19/3/3/9/78.

1 Introduction to LSP teaching
- history of development in Poland
- current tendencies

2 Characteristics of LSPs at a lexical level
- definition and characteristics of the term
- LSP terminology

3 Characteristics of LSPs at a grammatical level
- morphological and syntactic constructions

4 Textual characteristics of LSPs
- types of specialised texts and their functions
- characteristics of oral and written specialised texts

5 Group specificity and needs analysis in LSP class

6 Strategies and techniques for learning and teaching LSP

7 Educational applications of media and information technology in the teaching of LSP

8 Effectiveness of acquiring specialised terminology

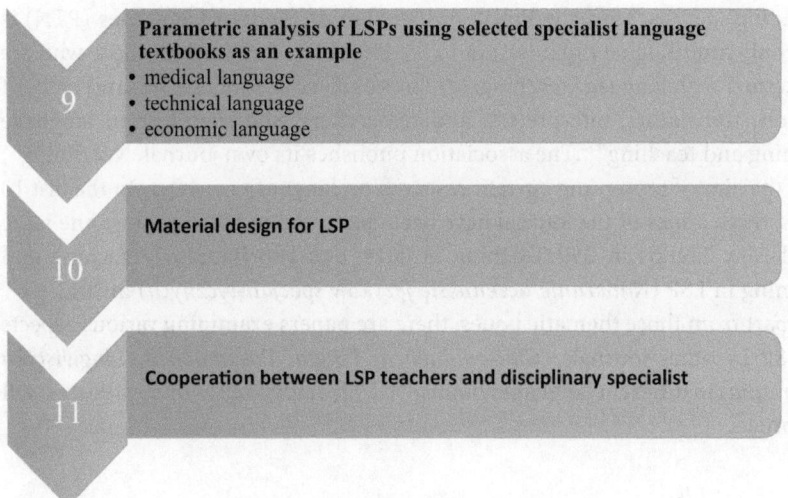

Figure 5. Syllabus of the LSP teaching course at Adam Mickiewicz University in Poznań, Poland

1.2.9. LSP conferences, associations and journals

In Poland, a separate association devoted to the promotion of LSP and bringing together academics researching the topic does not exist. However, the significance of the topic and interest in it are visible in the fact that, in recent years, previously existing foreign language associations have included the topic of LSP teaching and research in their conferences and journals.

Since 2015, 13 conferences on different aspects of LSP teaching have been organised by different Polish universities (in Łódź, Katowice, Poznań, Lublin, Rzeszów). A wide variety of aspects of LSP were discussed during these conferences, for example, the presence of LSPs in education programmes, development of language curricula for professional purposes at different stages of education, techniques and tools used in LSP teaching, evaluation and certification of skills in specialist languages, LSP teacher education and professional development, new trends in language teaching for vocational purposes, cooperation between education and employers, and current state and prospects for the development or national and European language policy guidelines. Two conferences (in Łódź and Rzeszów) have been organised on a regular basis. In Łódź there have been three editions of the conference (2016, 2017, 2021) and in Rzeszów four (2016, 2017, 2018, 2019).

There are no separate associations in Poland dedicated solely to the teaching of LSP. Among the organisations that deal with the subject of language teaching, including LSP teaching, the Polish Association of Modern Languages (PTN) is "the only multilingual organisation in the Republic of Poland for those who are concerned with language teaching: teachers of all educational levels and types of schools, translators, interpreters, and researchers who specialise in language learning and teaching"[32].The association publishes its own journal, Neofilolog[33], with the aim of presenting current research on language teaching. In the last 10 years, three issues of the journal have been dedicated to LSP teaching: one issue titled New Trends in LSP Teaching in 2018, and two issues of Teaching and Learning in LSP (*Nauczanie/uczenie się języków specjalistycznych*) in 2013.

Apart from those thematic issues, there are papers examining various aspects of LSP in other journals (*Glottodidactica, Lingua Posnaniensis, Lingwistyka stosowana*) in different languages published by leading Polish universities, as well as abroad.

1.3. Slovenia

1.3.1. Presentation

Slovenia is a country located in Central Europe, and lies between the Alps, the Pannonian Plain, and the Adriatic Sea. It neighbours Austria to the north, Italy to the west, Croatia to the east and south, and Hungary to the northeast. Its area covers 20,271 km^2. Its population is approximately 2.1 million. The capital city is Ljubljana.

According to the last population census of 2002, 83% of the citizens of Slovenia are of Slovene nationality, followed by Croats (2%) and Serbs (2%). Two autochthonous minorities with officially recognised rights and the right to education and the use of their language in public life live in Slovenia: the Italian minority in the littoral southwest region of Primorska (0.1% of the total population) and the Hungarian minority in the northeast region of Prekmurje (0.3% of the total population). Nationwide, the official language is Slovene, which is an inflectional language that belongs to the South Slavic group of Indo-European languages. Slovene is spoken as a mother language by 2.5 million speakers worldwide (Čuk, 2015).

After World War II, Slovenia was one of the six Yugoslav republics. It gained independence in 1990 after the disintegration of the Yugoslav state. Other important political and economic milestones include joining the EU in 2004, and

---

32 http://poltowneo.org/english/about-ptn.html.
33 https://pressto.amu.edu.pl/index.php/n.

the adoption of the European single currency Euro and joining the Schengen area in 2007.

Slovenia is a parliamentary democracy republic with a multi-party system. According to Eurostat, the GDP per capita was EUR 21,310 in 2021[34]. In 2021, services held a 56% share in the GDP, followed by industry (32%), and agriculture (2%)[35].

In Slovenia, there are three public universities, one private university, and several autonomous higher education institutions. Almost 30% of the population aged 15 or more has post-secondary education (Razpotnik, 2022).

1.3.2. Educational system

In Slovenia, the right to and freedom of education is a constitutional right, guaranteed by Article 57 of the Constitution of the Republic of Slovenia[36], according to which "The state shall create opportunities for citizens to obtain a proper education." In addition, primary education, enacted by the basic school (usually for children aged 6–15), is "compulsory and shall be financed by public funds".

The common legislative document which stipulates the provision, governance, and financing of education at all levels, from pre-school education in nursery schools to adult education, is the Organisation and Financing of Education Act[37]. Each level of education is then covered by specific acts, presented in Table 3.

Table 3. Legislative documents that regulate the educational system in Slovenia

Level of education	Act	Purpose
Pre-school education	Nursery schools Act	Preschool education provided by public and private nursery schools.
Basic school	Basic School Act	Basic education performed by public and private basic schools or as education at home.

---

34 https://ec.europa.eu/eurostat/databrowser/view/sdg_08_10/default/table.
35 https://www.statista.com/statistics/329073/share-of-economic-sectors-in-the-gdp-in-slovenia/.
36 https://www.us-rs.si/media/constitution.pdf.
37 http://www.pisrs.si/Pis.web/pregledPredpisa?id=ZAKO445.

Table 3 *(Continued)*

Level of education	Act	Purpose
Upper secondary general education	*Gimnazija* Act	Education in general and technical *gimnazija* schools (general upper secondary schools and general upper secondary schools with specialisation).
Short upper secondary vocational education, upper secondary vocational education, and upper secondary technical education	Vocational and Technical Education Act	Short vocational upper secondary education, upper secondary vocational education, and upper secondary technical education.
Short-cycle higher vocational education	Higher Vocational Education Act	Education for the acquisition and supplementation of state-approved higher vocational education, and the organisation of higher vocational colleges.
Higher education	Higher Education Act	Status of higher education institutions and requirements for the performance of higher education activities.
Adult education	Adult Education Act	Education, training and instruction of persons who have met their compulsory education requirement.

A simplified structure of the education system in Slovenia is presented in Figure 6. The system will be briefly described in terms of the goals that each level seeks to achieve (see Ministry of Education, Science and Sport of the Republic of Slovenia, 2019), with particular focus placed on the stages of the path that a future teacher of foreign languages (for specific purposes) would undertake.

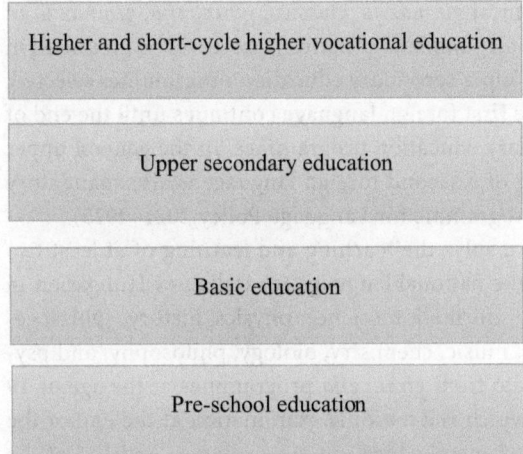

Figure 6. Structure of the education system in Slovenia (for details, see the Slovene Education System and Slovene Qualifications Framework[38])

Preschool education is dedicated to children from the age of one until they start basic education. Mostly at the age of six, children enter basic nine-year school education, which merges primary and lower secondary education in three three-year educational cycles. The main goals of basic school education seek to develop and foster the following abilities and traits in pupils: personal development, knowledge and skills in line with their interests and abilities, continuous education and life-long learning, sense of identity, cultural values, diversity, human rights, mother language and foreign language skills, sustainable development, responsibility and innovation, creativity, and entrepreneurship. According to the Resolution on the National Programme for Language Policy 2021–2025[39], "The teaching of the first foreign language is carried out from the second grade onwards within the compulsory part of the primary school curriculum. Optionally, however, pupils can learn it from the first grade onwards." (2021, p. 41) In addition, pupils "can learn an additional second foreign language from the second educational period onwards as an optional elective subject, and in the third educational period as a compulsory or optional elective subject." (idem, p. 41)

After the completion of basic school education, mostly at the age of 15, students may enrol in different upper secondary education programmes. Because future foreign language teachers would normally continue their educational path at four-year upper secondary general education institutions, called *gimnazija*

---

38 https://www.gov.si/en/topics/slovenski-solski-sistem-in-slovensko-ogrodje-kvalifikacij/.
39 https://jezikovna-politika.si/portfolio/resolution-on-the-national-programme-for-language-policy-2021-2025/.

(these include *gimnazija*, technical *gimnazija*, classical *gimnazija*, *gimnazija* of arts, *gimnazija* of economics, and *gimnazija* of sports), these will be presented in more detail. Regardless of the upper secondary education programmes selected, the compulsory learning of the first foreign language continues until the end of vocational and general secondary education programmes. In the general upper secondary school, the learning of a second foreign language is also mandatory (Resolution on the National Programme for Language Policy 2021–2025).

All *gimnazija* programmes involve the teaching and learning of at least two foreign languages, Slovene as the national language (or Italian or Hungarian in bilingual areas), mathematics, information science, physics, history, sports, geography, sociology, visual arts, music, chemistry, biology, philosophy, and psychology. Most students graduate from *gimnazija* programmes at the age of 19 with a general *matura* exam, which is a national examination at the end of the fourth year of upper secondary general education. According to Article 5 of the Matura Examination Act[40], a foreign language is a compulsory subject that students take. A successfully completed *matura* examination allows them to enrol in higher education professional and academic study programmes.

Following the Bologna Reform of Higher Education, which defines the European Higher Education Area (EHEA)[41], the Slovene higher education system is organised in three study cycles (with the exception of integrated master's degree courses, such as architecture, and the studies of some other disciplines, such as medicine):
- first-cycle (bachelor's degree) professional and academic study programmes,
- second-cycle (master's or integrated master's degree) study programmes, and
- third-cycle doctoral degree study programmes.

The registry of higher education institutions in Slovenia[42] lists 112 institutions. Among these, the institutions that provide pre-service education for future foreign language teachers at post-basic education institutions and, as a consequence, LSP teachers, are located at the three Slovene public universities:
- the University of Ljubljana[43] (Faculty of Arts),
- the University of Maribor[44] (Faculty of Arts), and
- the University of Primorska[45] (Faculty of Humanities).

---

40 http://www.pisrs.si/Pis.web/pregledPredpisa?id=ZAKO2064.
41 http://ehea.info/.
42 https://www.gov.si/teme/evs-evidenca-visokosolskih-zavodov-in-studijskih-programov/.
43 https://www.uni-lj.si/university/.
44 https://www.um.si/en/home-page/.
45 https://www.upr.si/en.

In addition, all three universities have faculties of education that provide education for future foreign language teachers for young learners in basic education. This means that unless they have completed their education abroad, all foreign language teachers in Slovenia teaching beyond basic education, including LSP teachers, are graduates from the Faculty of Arts of the University of Ljubljana or the University of Maribor, or the Faculty of Humanities of the University of Primorska.

1.3.3. Language policy

In Slovenia, the national official language is Slovene. However, "in those municipalities where Italian or Hungarian national communities reside, Italian or Hungarian shall also be official languages." (Article 11 of the Constitution of the Republic of Slovenia)

An important milestone was reached in 2021, when Slovenia became the first country that included sign languages and the languages of the deaf-blind in its Constitution (Article 62.a). The main document that addresses language policy in Slovenia is the Resolution on the National Programme for Language Policy 2021–2025[46]. The main objective of the language policy is to provide speakers of Slovene with adequate education and development in the use of the Slovene language (or Italian and Hungarian as the constitutionally guaranteed mother languages in the bilingual municipalities where these two autochthonous communities live) so that they can efficiently use their mother tongue in their personal and professional lives. In addition, the citizens of Slovenia are to be provided with opportunities to raise their awareness of the importance of multilingualism and intercultural communication. As a result, "the teaching of the first foreign language is carried out from the second grade onwards within the compulsory part of the primary school curriculum. Optionally, however, pupils can learn it from the first grade onwards. Compulsory learning of the first foreign language is continued after primary school until the completion of secondary general and vocational education programmes (excluding lower vocational education programmes). In their programmes, schools choose between English and German, but they can also offer and carry out courses of both languages." (Resolution on the National Programme for Language Policy 2021–2025, 2021, p. 41). In addition, in bilingual municipalities Italian and Hungarian are taught as second (i.e., languages of the environment) and not as foreign languages. At the higher education level, numerous study programmes include the teaching of languages for specific purposes, mostly English. In 2016, more than 84% of Slovenes spoke at

---

46 https://jezikovna-politika.si/wp-content/uploads/2021/09/ReNPJP2021-2025-ENG.pdf.

least one foreign language while approximately 33% said they spoke at least two foreign languages (Svetlin Kastelic, 2017).

1.3.4. LSP teachers – legal regulations

To understand the qualifications that need to be met to become a foreign language teacher at a Slovene secondary school or in a higher education institution, several legislative documents need to be consulted and their content integrated.

The qualifications required to apply for a particular position in the public sector, including education, are set by the Organisation and Financing of Education Act[47]. Foreign language teachers belong under the umbrella of general subject teachers. According to Articles 96 (for vocational and professional schools) and 97 (for *gimnazija*) of this Act, general subject teachers "shall have the educational qualification of a second cycle study programme, or the level of the educational qualification of study programmes corresponding, in accordance with the law, to the educational qualification of the second cycle in the relevant field, as well as the pedagogical-andragogical educational qualification." In other words, they need to have relevant qualifications in their specific field (e.g., linguistics and literature) as well as in teaching methodology. Moreover, Article 100 states that "A staff member who has not completed a higher education study programme which also includes a pedagogical, pedagogical-andragogical or special pedagogical educational qualification shall obtain it by completing a relevant officially recognised supplementary study programme." For foreign language teachers this means completing a second-cycle master's degree study programme for teachers or foreign languages or, alternatively, completing a 'non-teaching' second-cycle degree programme in linguistics and literature plus an additional foreign language teaching methodology programme.

That the first condition to apply for a position of foreign language teacher is a second-cycle (or equivalent) degree in foreign linguistics and/or literature (and not a degree in other fields) is set out by Articles 9–15 of the Rules on the Level of Education of Teachers and Other Professionals in Educational Programmes of General Upper Secondary Schools (*gimnazije*)[48] and Article 4 of the Rules on the Education of Teachers and Other Expert Workers in Vocational and Professional Education[49].

---

[47] http://www.pisrs.si/Pis.web/pregledPredpisa?id=ZAKO445.
[48] http://www.pisrs.si/Pis.web/pregledPredpisa?id=PRAV12514.
[49] http://pisrs.si/Pis.web/pregledPredpisa?id=PRAV14708.

Given that according to Article 58 of the Constitution of the Republic of Slovenia[50]: "State universities and state institutions of higher education shall be autonomous.", the situation for higher education foreign language teachers is slightly different.

According to the Catalogue of Positions in the Public Sector[51], teachers of linguistics, literature, and LSP can take the positions of full professor, associate professor, assistant professor, and teaching assistant (teaching at first-cycle academic degree studies, and second- and third-cycle degree studies), and senior lecturer, and lecturer (teaching at first-cycle professional degree studies). In addition, a specific position has been created for language teachers, both for general linguistics courses and LSP: lector. Together with full professors, associate professors, and assistant professors, lectors make up the group of higher education teachers and can teach at all levels of higher education. While to hold the position of full professor, associate professor, or assistant professor a doctoral degree is an essential condition, the requirements to be awarded the title of lector are a relevant second-cycle degree (or equivalent), three years of teaching experience, and at least three months of continuous professional or teaching activity in "a linguistic environment where the language in question is naturally used" (Article 76 of the Criteria for Appointment to the Titles of University Teachers, Researchers and Associates at the University of Ljubljana[52]). In other words, this means that an LSP teacher may teach at the third-cycle degree level without holding a degree equivalent to that their students are pursuing. Moreover, there are some instances in which LSP teachers are still employed as skills teachers (another category for public employees recognised by the Catalogue of Positions in the Public Sector), which significantly affects their salaries and status within the teaching community (see the following subchapter on the status of LSP teachers in Slovenia).

Importantly, what all examined levels of education – vocational, secondary, and higher – have in common is that no legislative document valid in the Republic of Slovenia defines any specific requirements for applying for the position of LSP teacher. This means that at the political level it is assumed that a second-cycle (or equivalent) degree in linguistics and literature combined with a general language teaching methodology course (or degree) is sufficient for effective foreign language teaching in specific contexts.

---

50 https://www.us-rs.si/media/constitution.pdf.
51 http://www.pportal.gov.si/FDMN/index.html.
52 https://www.uni-lj.si/o_univerzi_v_ljubljani/organizacija__pravilniki_in_porocila/predpisi_statut_ul_in_pravilniki/20130711111373294/.

1.3.5. Status of LSP teachers

One of the main findings of a research study into the status of LSP teachers at Slovene universities published by Jurkovič et al. (2008) almost fifteen years ago was that their status significantly differed between institutions, which could in part be attributed to the lack of clarity of the legislative documents on one hand, and on the autonomy of public universities (Article 58 of the Constitution of the Republic of Slovenia[53]) on the other hand.

The autonomy of public universities implies that each institution is in charge of their own job classification, which they, as an entity governed by public law, need to have and that "shall include at least a description of the tasks and conditions for holding each post" (see Article 21 of the Public Employees Act[54]). The job classification needs to comply with the provisions of the superordinate Collective Agreement for the Education Sector in the Republic of Slovenia[55]. The fact that each institution may define their own job classification has resulted in the fact that at Slovene universities LSP teachers can actually hold any of the following 12 job positions: higher education teacher – lector (further divided into lector with a doctoral degree, lector with a master's degree, and lector), higher education teacher (these include the positions of full professor, associate professor, and assistant professor), higher education teacher – lecturer (senior lecturer and lecturer), skills teacher, and teaching assistant (including a teaching assistant with a doctoral degree, a teaching assistant with a master's degree, and a teaching assistant).

Importantly, the position (defined by the job classification of each institution) does not necessarily match the academic title that an LSP teacher holds. This technically means that an LSP teacher that has been awarded the title of associate professor, for instance, can hold the position of skills teacher. The position, and not the academic title, then results in the status at their institution (including membership in faculty senate bodies or various committees etc.), their salaries, and weekly workloads, for instance 6 teaching hours for a full professor, and 20 teaching hours for a skills teacher (see for instance Article 5 of the Criteria for the Workload Evaluation of Higher Education Teachers and Associates of the Faculty of Arts of the University of Maribor[56]).

On the other hand, the status of LSP teachers in vocational and secondary education seems to be less complex. LSP teachers have the same status as all other teachers of general subjects. During their careers, they will start as novice

---

53 https://www.us-rs.si/media/constitution.pdf.
54 http://pisrs.si/Pis.web/pregledPredpisa?id=ZAKO3177.
55 http://pisrs.si/Pis.web/pregledPredpisa?id=KOLP19.
56 https://ff.um.si/wp-content/uploads/Merila-za-vrednotenje-dela-visoko%C5%A1olskih-u%C4%8Diteljev-in-sodelavcev-FF-UM.pdf.

teachers but can then advance to the title (and position) of teacher mentor, teacher advisor, and teacher counsellor. This will have a positive effect on their status and salary but not on other job-related responsibilities nor weekly workload.

1.3.6. LSP provision in higher education

In Slovenia, LSP classes are provided for students in upper secondary technical schools, short-cycle higher vocational education, higher education, and language schools. In this section we will briefly focus on the provision of LSP classes in Slovene higher education.

LSP teaching in Slovene higher education is based on a long tradition. In the 1990s, with a few exceptions, most higher education institutions offered LSP in their programmes (Djurić, 1999). Unfortunately, the Bologna Reform had a detrimental effect on LSP provision in Slovenia. At many higher education institutions, the number of hours dedicated to LSP were reduced, and in some cases LSP provision was entirely discontinued. Thus, LSP teaching in the Slovene higher education area remains characterised by important systemic inconsistencies (Jurkovič & Djurić, 2008). As Djurić noted already in 1999, LSP provision still lacks consistency in terms of, for instance, the length of implementation (number of contact hours), beginning of implementation, and most importantly, status of the LSP course: compulsory, elective, or absent.

To provide an example, Tables 4 and 5 present LSP provision for students of first-cycle degree studies at the Faculty of Maritime Studies and Transport of the University of Ljubljana for the following study programmes:
- first-cycle professional degree (180 ECTS) in Marine Engineering,
- first-cycle professional degree (180 ECTS) in Nautical Studies,
- first-cycle professional degree (180 ECTS) in Traffic Technology and Transport Logistics, and
- first-cycle academic degree (180 ECTS) in Transport Technology and Logistics.

Table 4. LSP provision at the Faculty of Maritime Studies and Transport of the University of Ljubljana (Maritime Department)

	Marine Engineering		Nautical Studies	
LSP course title	Maritime English	English for Marine Engineering	Maritime English	English for Nautical Studies
LSP course status	Compulsory	Compulsory	Compulsory	Compulsory
Semester	1	4	1	4
Number of contact hours	75	75	75	75
ECTS	5	5	5	5
Intended course outcomes (example)	Students will be able to compare vessel details.	Students will be able to understand ship engine operation and maintenance manuals.	Students will be able to compare vessel details.	Students will be able to use English in written and oral form to understand meteorological information and messages concerning ship safety and operations.

Table 5. LSP provision at the Faculty of Maritime Studies and Transport of the University of Ljubljana (Transport Technology Department)

	Traffic Technology and Transport Logistics		Transport Technology and Logistics	
LSP course title	Professional English 1	Professional English 2	Professional English I	Professional English II
LSP course status	Compulsory	Compulsory	Compulsory	Elective
Semester	3	4	3	5
Number of contact hours	65	65	67	70
ECTS	5	5	5	5
Intended course outcomes (examples)	Students will be able to understand professional texts in traffic technology and transport logistics.	Students will be able to write business emails, with particular reference to traffic technology and transport logistics activities.	Students will be able to distinguish between academic and professional text genres.	Students will be able to write a researched essay.

1.3.7. Subjects supporting LSP teacher education at universities

Although in Slovenia there are no accredited study programmes nor modules at any level of higher education that would be specifically dedicated to the pre-service education of LSP teachers (John et al., 2023; Podgoršek et al., 2021), there are a number of first- and second-cycle degree courses in linguistics and general language teaching methodology that provide pre-service LSP teachers with the foundations for their future LSP teaching careers. In this way, the needs that they share with future general language teachers are catered for. These include, for instance, teaching skills, motivation and autonomy, and classroom management (see Jurkovič et al., 2023).

An overview of courses provided to students of the second-cycle degree study programme in English Studies – Single Teacher Education Course at the Department of English of the Faculty of Arts at the University of Ljubljana, taken as an example, reveals that numerous LSP teacher professional development needs (see Jurkovič et al., 2023) are catered for by general English language teaching methodology courses (University of Ljubljana, 2022). During the Adult Education course, for instance, students learn about the obstacles to, and reasons and motivation for adult education. The Didactics syllabus includes the examination of the didactic phases of the teaching process. Another example is the Language Competences course, which requires students to read expert texts. Moreover, the Methods and Techniques of Teaching English course includes a section on ESP but also discusses other topics that are relevant to future LSP teachers, for instance learner autonomy and the role of instructional materials. The course titled The Fundamentals of English Language Teaching enables students to learn about the development of language skills. Last but not least, the Psychology for Teachers course also focuses on communication and classroom management. These topics, although they are covered by general language teaching methodology courses, are undoubtedly of utmost importance to any LSP teacher as well.

1.3.8. LSP teacher education

In Slovenia, there are no accredited study programmes nor modules at any level of higher education that would be specifically dedicated to the pre-service education of LSP teachers and would thus prepare them to efficiently cope with the challenges of LSP teaching and research (John et al., 2023; Podgoršek et al., 2021). However, each of the three Slovene public universities provides one elective course in LSP teaching.

At the Department of English at the Faculty of Arts of the University of Ljubljana, students of the second-cycle degree study programme in English

Studies may opt for the elective course titled Teaching English for Specific Purposes. The main objectives of the 3 ECTS course are to provide an overview of the main developments in ESP teaching, including teaching methodology, needs analysis, materials and course design, and assessment[57].

Similarly, the Department of English and American Studies at the Faculty of Arts of the University of Maribor offers a 3 ECTS elective course in Teaching English for Specific Purposes, which can be selected by students of the second-cycle degree study programme in Teaching English. The course "aims to prepare students for planning and teaching English in different professions and vocation-related options" (University of Maribor, 2022, p. 86) through the implementation of a syllabus that focuses on the historical and theoretical background of ESP, needs analysis, evaluation (of syllabuses, coursebooks, and ESP teaching materials), syllabus design, lesson planning, materials development, and assessment and testing.

Last but not least, the curriculum of the second-cycle degree programme in Italian Studies provided by the Department of Italian Studies at the Faculty of Humanities of the University of Primorska comprises a 3 ECTS elective course in Didactics of Languages for Specific Purposes. The syllabus of this course includes an introduction to LSP didactics, LSP learning and teaching, teaching resources and aids, macro- and micro-articulation of learning contents, evaluation and self-evaluation of LSP knowledge, and application of theory in practice (University of Primorska, 2022).

1.3.9. LSP conferences, associations and journals

In Slovenia, the association that provides a meeting point for LSP teachers at different levels of education and supports their continuous professional development is the Slovene Association of LSP Teachers[58]. The main activities of the Association include the regular organisation of national and international conferences, a regular provision of workshops in various areas relevant to LSP teaching and research (corpus analysis, academic paper writing, use of referencing tools, etc.), the promotion of research activities of their members, the creation of glossaries pertinent to different fields, the development of cooperation with educational and ministerial institutions in Slovenia, and the networking with partner associations in Slovenia and abroad (for instance IATEFL Slovenia[59],

---

57 https://www.ff.uni-lj.si/en/node/180252.
58 http://eng.sdutsj.si.
59 https://www.iatefl.si/.

the Association of LSP Teachers at Higher Education Institutions[60] from Croatia, and the International Federation of Language Teacher Associations[61]).

Since its establishment in 1997, the Slovene Association of LSP Teachers has organised several national and international conferences. The first international conference titled Languages for Specific Purposes: Opportunities and Challenges of Teaching and Research was held in Rimske terme, Slovenia, in 2017 to celebrate the 20th anniversary of the Association. Since then, two more international conferences were held: the 2020 event was organised online while the 2023 again brought together LSP researchers and teachers at an in-person event in Rimske terme. In addition to the conferences organised by the Slovene Association of LSP Teachers, the University of Maribor regularly holds international LSP conferences titled The Importance of Learning Professional Foreign Languages for Communication between Cultures.

LSP teachers and researchers can publish their papers in several Slovene journals dedicated to general linguistic and educational research. However, the Slovene Association of LSP Teachers is the publisher of Scripta Manent[62], a peer-reviewed open-access journal that is specifically dedicated to the publication of papers that strive to bridge theory and practice in the LSP teaching profession, and thus contribute to the professional development of its readers in the national and international LSP community. Since its establishment in 2007, 16 volumes with more than a hundred research papers, teaching reports, and book reviews have been published. In addition, papers presented at LSP conferences held in Slovenia are published in dedicated conference proceedings. The first is Inter Alia[63], a publication series of the Slovene Association of LSP Teachers with proceedings from their national and international conferences. The second is the proceedings with papers presented at the above-mentioned LSP conferences organised by the University of Maribor (for instance, Vičič et al. 2018).

1.4. Synthesis

In this chapter, we have provided an overview of those aspects of the Polish and Slovene background that contribute to the education and professional development of future pre-service and existing in-service LSP teachers. Given that both examined countries are EU members, it was to be expected that the edu-

---

60 https://unjsvu.hr/en/.
61 https://fiplv.com/.
62 https://scriptamanent.sdutsj.edus.si/ScriptaManent.
63 http://sdutsj.si/inter-alia.

cational context would be characterised by numerous similarities and only a few disparities. Both will be highlighted in this section.

First of all, both countries are parliamentary democracies and members of the EU. However, they significantly differ in terms of size, number of native speakers of the national language, geographic and geopolitical positions, and last but not least historical backgrounds. All of these factors have had an impact on the differences in the educational systems, linguistic contexts, and language policies.

The political support for the learning of foreign languages is evidenced by the fact that the teaching of the first foreign language, English in both cases, starts at the age of seven (first grade in Poland and second grade in Slovenia, where pupils start attending primary school one year earlier, i.e., at the age of six). In Slovenia, however, the presence of two autochthonous minorities means that the pupils living in bilingual areas will start learning the language of the environment (Italian or Hungarian; or Slovene as the language of the environment for native speakers of Italian or Hungarian) at the age of six. This means that at the age of seven, these children will be learning their mother language, the language of the environment, and English as a foreign language. For children living in non-bilingual areas, the second foreign language (mostly German) can become an optional elective subject. In addition, the political support to foreign language learning is corroborated by the presence of a foreign language as a compulsory subject in the national external examinations (i.e., *matura* examinations) in both countries. In Poland and Slovenia, the learning of a second foreign language is mandatory in general upper secondary schools.

A significant difference between the two countries was found in terms of language policy. While in Poland there is one official language, in the Slovene bilingual areas there are two. In addition, it seems that in Poland the number of speakers of one foreign language and of more than one foreign language seems to be significantly lower than in Slovenia. This can be attributed to the factors mentioned above (size, number of native speakers of the national language, geographic and geopolitical positions, historical backgrounds) but most probably also to the ethnic origin of the majority of the population: 95% citizens of Poland have Polish origins whereas 83% citizens of Slovenia have Slovene origins.

To become a foreign language teacher in Poland one does not necessarily have to be a holder of a degree in linguistics and/or literature because a certificate of proficiency or advanced standing in the relevant foreign language combined with a teacher education programme may mean the beginning of someone's career as a foreign language teacher. In Slovenia, on the other hand, a degree in linguistics (including translation studies) and/or literature combined with a teacher education programme is an essential condition for becoming a foreign language teacher. It seems that the policies in both countries rely on the assumption that the completion of a teacher education programme for foreign language teaching automatically indicates that a person has been prepared for LSP teaching, too. However, there is a significant difference that may be at first glance overlooked. In Poland, the completion of a subject on LSP teaching is a compulsory component of foreign language teacher education. On the other hand, in Slovenia courses in LSP teaching are provided by all institutions that provide education for future language teachers but they are in all three cases elective. This consequently means that in Slovenia LSP teachers may begin their teaching careers without any background knowledge, skills, or competences for LSP teaching. It has to be noted, however, that first-cycle and second-cycle degree studies include a number of subjects that support specialist linguistic knowledge and methodological preparation. This, however, excludes the specialist professional knowledge related to a specific LSP field.

The Bologna Reform of higher education seems to have had a different impact in the two countries. While in Poland the number of LSP classes which were treated as elective was reduced in favour of compulsory courses, in Slovenia the process seems to have been reversed; i.e. in several cases the LSP classes which were treated as compulsory became elective. In both countries, however, the number of hours for LSP teaching was reduced.

The status of LSP teachers in both countries seems to be somewhat similar. Most importantly, holding a PhD does not seem to be a precondition to becoming a higher education LSP teacher while the position does not necessarily match the academic title that an LSP teacher holds.

Finally, LSP seems to be receiving increasing attention from LSP researchers and teachers in both countries, which is evidenced by the number of conferences either specifically dealing with LSP or including various aspects of LSP teaching and research as conference thematic areas. Nevertheless, it seems that the teaching and research needs of Polish LSP teachers are catered for by associations and journals that are not exclusively dedicated to LSP teaching but foreign languages in general. In Slovenia, on the other hand, the Slovene Association of LSP Teachers is dedicated to LSP teaching and research, which can be published in *Scripta Manent*, a journal dedicated to the publication of LSP research.

2. Introduction to LSP

2.1. Introduction

Teaching LSP still evokes numerous doubts, especially among novice teachers or people not entirely familiar with the subject. On the one hand, those doubts result from the still existing gaps in research on LSP teaching, and on the other hand, from the lack of a clear definition and didactic-methodological criteria defining the difference between LGP and LSP teaching.

Therefore, this chapter addresses the main aspects of LSP teaching. The starting point for reflection is a short history of LSP development and an attempt to formulate a definition of LSP for the needs of this publication. The next subchapter thematises the specificity of the creation of LSP syllabuses and curricula in comparison to LGP syllabuses and curricula. Then, efficient LSP materials design is explained and accompanied by methodological recommendations for their implementation in LSP classrooms. The final subchapter is dedicated to LSP assessment.

2.2. Definition

In order to be able to understand the premises on which the subsequent subchapters are built, LSP first needs to be clearly described and defined.

The development of LSP, in particular in English, can be traced back to the period following World War II when the global community experienced intense scientific, technical, and economic progress, and thus the necessity for a common language used for communication in specific situations and disciplines. In addition, the development in the fields of linguistics and foreign language acquisition and learning, supported by educational psychology, significantly contributed to the later emergence of the awareness that we need to focus on both how people learn as well as what they learn to become efficient users of the language used in specific communication events (Hutchinson & Waters, 1987).

In fact, LSP is founded on the principle of specificity (Hyland, 2016). This means that LSP encompasses domains of language knowledge and skills that would not be parts of the communicative repertoire of an educated average native speaker of that language, which is the case of most topics covered by LGP courses (Basturkmen, 2010; Tudor, 1997). For example, an educated native speaker that is not acquainted with the world of maritime affairs would not be familiar with the structure and content of the distress call and message transmitted by vessels in distress situations. On the other hand, an educated native speaker would be able to discuss the general advantages and disadvantages of living in urban or rural environments, which is a frequent topic of courses designed for LGP teaching and learning. Moreover, the specificity of LSP also lies in the specific language that is used in the target discipline, i.e., how language features in the discipline, how specific vocabulary is used in the discipline, and which genres and texts types are typically used to communicate disciplinary content (Bocanegra-Valle & Basturkmen, 2019). What is therefore key for LSP teaching is the teaching and learning of the understanding of how language is used in specific contexts. This entails, at least, a level of knowledge, skills, and/or competences in discipline-specific vocabulary (i.e., terminology), and typical genres and the rhetorical structure and context of discipline-specific texts (Bocanegra-Valle & Basturkmen, 2019). LSP thus reaches beyond the general language knowledge required in LGP teaching and learning.

LSP is a generic term for a variety of subcategories that define in which circumstances and for which purposes a foreign language is learnt. Therefore, it is "an approach to language learning, which is based on learner need." (Hutchinson & Waters, 1987, p. 19) It can broadly be defined as "the teaching and research of language in relation to the communicative needs of speakers of a second language in facing a particular workplace, academic, or professional context." (Basturkmen & Elder, 2004, p. 672) Therefore, what is key to LSP is that the objective of LSP learners is to learn how to communicate effectively in a particular setting. In order to enable them to achieve this objective, the language and genres need to be extracted from their professional or academic domains (Paltridge & Starfield, 2013).

A frequently quoted detailed description of LSP was provided by Dudley-Evans and StJohn (1998), whose definition relies on three absolute and four variable characteristics. The absolute characteristics of LSP are that its design is such to meet the learners' specific needs, that the methodology and activities it uses are based on the disciplinary domain that LSP is connected with, and that the language taught needs to be appropriate for carrying out these activities. On the other hand, the four variable characteristics are that LSP may be linked to several different disciplines or tailored to specific domains, that it may rely on different teaching and learning methodology than languages for general purposes (LGP), that the learners are mostly adults, and that their pre-existing general foreign language proficiency usually is not basic but rather intermediate or advanced.

The world of LSP can be divided into two broad categories (see e.g., Basturkmen, 2010; Charles & Pecorari, 2016; Hutchinson & Waters, 1997), the framework of which will largely define the target and learner needs, the learning objectives, the teaching and learning materials and methodology, and evaluation. The first category concerns languages for academic purposes (LAP), which refers to the foreign language used to carry out activities related to academic contexts. In most academic contexts, this is realised through English for Academic Purposes (EAP) where English acts as the *lingua franca* of the academic world (Mauranen et al., 2010). LAP can be further divided into languages for general academic purposes (LGAP) and languages for specific academic purposes (LSAP). If LGAP focuses on the academic language that several disciplines have in common (e.g., music education, civil engineering, and veterinary science), LSAP focuses on the teaching of those features that make one academic discipline or set of disciplines different from another (e.g., focus is placed on the rhetorical structure and discipline-specific terminology of academic papers in logistics and not all academic papers in general). The second category consists of languages for professional purposes (LPP), which prepares the learners for communication in professional non-academic contexts. LPP can be further subdivided into languages for general professional purposes (LGPP; e.g., Maritime English designed as an introductory course for students of navigation as well as students of marine engineering), and languages for specific professional purposes (LSPP; e.g., maritime communication that will only be used in their future professional contexts by students of navigation but not by students of marine engineering). The teaching and learning of LPP can be found at different levels of education, for instance in secondary technical education, higher education, or adult education through LSP courses (e.g., a language course in business English for a pharmaceutical company). On the other hand, the teaching and learning of LAP is typical of higher education institutions. More and more frequently LAP courses, in particular academic writing in English, are provided to native speakers of English as well, for instance by the University of Bath[64] and University of Sunderland[65], among many others.

LSP shares some features with content and language integrated learning (CLIL) whereas the teaching and learning of ESP also partially overlaps with English as a Medium of Instruction (EMI). However, LSP is also inherently and significantly different from both. In terms of LSP teaching and learning, Dudley-

---

64 https://www.bath.ac.uk/catalogues/2020-2021/el/EL00708.html.
65 https://www.sunderland.ac.uk/study/short-courses-cpd/eap-academic-writing-native-speakers-english/.

Evans and St John (1998) make a distinction between real content and carrier content, the latter being the specific topic or context that is used to teach and learn the real content, i.e., the discipline-specific language. On the other hand, CLIL can be defined as "the teaching and learning of both language and subject areas (e.g., science, mathematics, etc.) in the same classroom, at the same time" (Barwell, 2005, p. 143). Because of the role of English as the *lingua franca* of higher education (Mauranen et al., 2010), numerous higher education institutions in countries where English is not the national language provide degree courses where English is used as EMI (Dearden, 2014) to attract international students or provide competitive advantages (i.e., the English language competence) to the local students. The main premise underlying EMI is that the foreign language will be acquired incidentally by studying the disciplinary content in this language. This means that EMI does not imply a formal focus on the learning of the foreign language but relies instead on the principles of incidental language acquisition as defined by Hulstijn (2003). The continuum between a focus placed on language and a focus placed on content of programmes that integrate and merge content and language teaching and learning briefly presented above, i.e., EMI, CLIL, and LSP, presented in Figure 7, was adapted from Thompson and McKinley (2018).

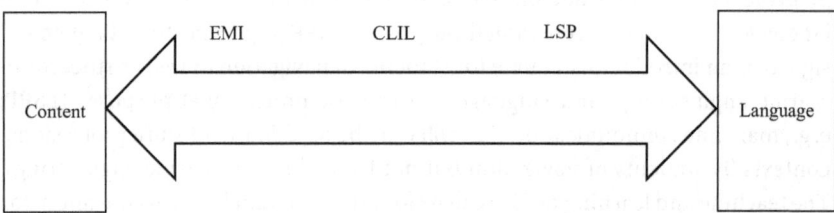

Figure 7. EMI, CLIL, and LSP placed on a continuum of programmes that integrate content and language (adapted from Thompson & McKinley, 2018)

Based on what has been said so far, it can be claimed that language learning based on learner need is a concept that lies at the core of LSP (Basturkmen, 2010). In addition, language learning based on learner need provides the foundations for the four pillars of LSP (Figure 8): needs analysis, learning objectives, materials and methods, and evaluation (Anthony, 2018).

First, needs analysis is conducted to gain an insight into the learners' target needs in terms of the language, genres, and knowledge, skills and/or competences that they need, or will need to efficiently communicate through language in the target situation, into the views of the different stakeholders' expectations, and into the learners' learning needs (i.e., which needs have to be met for the process of learning to take place). Second, based on the identification of the learners' target and learning needs, the learning objectives are designed.

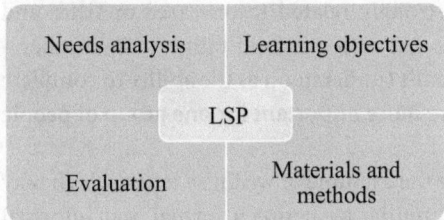

Figure 8. Four pillars of LSP (Anthony, 2018)

These will match the findings of the needs analysis process in terms of register, discourse, genre, learning, and metacognition. Third, the teaching and learning materials and the adopted teaching and learning methodology allow the learners to understand the target setting in which the language that they are learning is used. The materials and methodology also help learners to incidentally and formally build and actively use their foreign language skills, and develop a positive emotional attitude to the foreign language skills being learnt. The fourth LSP pillar is evaluation, which includes learner assessment (diagnostic, formative, and summative) as well as course evaluation (Anthony, 2018). These pillars of LSP will provide a broad framework for the discussion of LSP-specific elements in dedicated subchapters below.

2.3. Needs analysis in LSP

As mentioned above, Anthony (2018) defines needs analysis as one of the key pillars of LSP teaching, next to learning objectives, materials and methods, and evaluation, underlining its importance in designing an efficient and target oriented curriculum.

To further highlight the significance of needs for LSP teaching, it is worth analysing the definition provided for ESP by Anthony (2018, p. 11), where needs are mentioned several times:

> English for Specific Purposes (ESP) is an approach to language teaching that targets the current and/or future <u>academic or occupational needs</u>[66] of learners, focuses on the necessary language, genres, and skills to address these needs, and assists learners in <u>meeting these needs</u> through the use of general and/or discipline-specific teaching materials and methods.

Interestingly, not all language needs are LSP needs although they aim at achieving a certain communicative goal. To put it more precisely, "ESP needs are (...) non-linguistic needs that have a linguistic component" (Anthony, 2018, p. 10),

---

66 Highlights made by the authors' of the publication.

which means there are needs more strongly related to one area or field, and resulting from a particular task connected with one field rather than another – the same way that there are language skills (understood as the ability to complete a specific communicative task) that are more important for one group of people than another.

Medrea and Rus (2012, p. 1167) give the example of writing a letter, which may be a general language need, but differentiating between formal and informal register "is one frequent complaint that comes from employers who can no longer afford to have employees whose learning on-the-job involves basic language skills." In that way, the authors highlight that students should first learn the general language skills, in order to adequately implement the specific terminology and discourse which are needed in their workplace.

Ronaldo and Pamungkas (2020) name three kinds of needs analysis necessary for designing LSP teaching materials:
- Target Situational Analysis, whose main goal is to identify learners' language requirements in a professional setting. Hutchinson and Waters (1987) also differentiate between necessities (needs determined by demands of target situation), lacks (determined by particular learners) and wants within target needs.
- Learning Needs Analysis, aimed at describing learner expectations, beliefs, motivation and learning styles concerning the language being learned, and
- Present Situational Analysis, helping to identify the weaknesses and strengths in the language skills of learners.

Target needs can be divided into academic and occupational needs. Academic needs refer to the learning setting of schools and universities, and the target group representing academic needs are students or pupils. Occupational needs refer to a work setting, and the groups that possess them are employees and employers first (Anthony, 2018), but more and more frequently these needs also concern university authorities and course designers (Gajewska et al., 2020).

Therefore, the classification of needs is closely related to the target group. Bocanegra-Valle (2016, p. 560) differentiates three levels of participants in the context of EAP:

> "1st level: primary stakeholders (present and past students) and EAP teachers,
> 2nd level: disciplinary teachers, educational authorities, policy makers, decision takers, faculty administrators, applied linguists, and
> 3rd level: professionals, sponsors, employers, and company representatives."

The selection of specific learning content is determined by the empirically verifiable needs of a given group of learners in terms of professional communication. These needs should be constantly reviewed, and reflected in the competence profiles of the graduates. As a rule, they should also correspond to the expectations of potential employers (Szerszeń, 2014).

Basturkmen (2010) and Bocanegra-Valle (2016) differentiate two kinds of target needs analysis: first-generation and second-generation analysis. The first category refers to the analysis of the target situation that the target learner group is dealing with or wants to enter through successful communication. The analysis comprises not only the situation itself but also the potential language use. Other factors belonging to the first-generation analysis group are the analysis of individual learners (their perception, wants and needs) and a teaching context analysis (analysis of the teaching environment). The second group of needs analysis tasks comprises task-based analyses consisting of the identification of target tasks, language use for the target tasks, and genre analysis. Also Lambert (2010) identified task-based language needs, explaining that for learners in a professional setting, the communicative tasks that they may perform are much more complex than the vocabulary or grammar they are able to employ.

Genre analysis is worth mentioning here, which is a needs analysis tool that provides deeper insights into the language used in target contexts. According to Hyland (2007, p. 149), "Genre refers to abstract, socially recognised ways of using language." Moreover, genres occur in predictable sequences, informing about the patterns and language resources needed for completion of a communication goal.

In addition to target needs, we also identify learning needs. These are gaps in individual knowledge or skills identified on the basis of comparison with the requirements needed to complete a task (Knowles et al., 2011). Learning needs are established through the process of learning needs analysis. The most popular tool for learning needs analysis are learner questionnaires. Brown (2016) and Huhta et al. (2013) cite their advantages as being quick, low-cost, easy to repeat, and efficient.

However, the questions need to be well-thought through beforehand. Anthony (2018) suggests some possible questions for a learning needs analysis survey to be completed by the learners, such as questions about their first language, age, gender, nationality, level of English, learning styles and preferences, reasons for taking the course, the knowledge and skills that they currently do not yet have, and so on.

Although learning needs are undoubtedly an important element of needs analysis, they are not sufficient to prepare learners well for professional situations. It is therefore worth taking into account the views of many stakeholders (Anthony, 2018) and different types of needs. This means that needs analysis should start from establishing the purpose of study and describing the target group. At this stage, the identification of possible limitations should also be conducted. The next stage consists in collecting, analysing, and interpreting the collected data. The final stage is determining the objectives and turning the identified needs into materials, strategies and so on (see Bocanegra-Valle, 2016).

Turning to the needs analysis process, Rossi et al. (2004, p. 3) describe it as "the means by which an evaluator determines whether there is a need for a program, and if so, what programme services are most appropriate to that end." According to Anthony (2018), needs analysis should address the questions of how, where, when, and why. A needs analysis can apply different data collection methods and resources, for example (see Anthony, 2018): literature reviews, questionnaires and surveys with learners, instructors, observations, genre analysis, analysis of learner language and target language.

The results of needs analysis provide the foundations for course design (Flowerdew, 2013) (Figure 9).

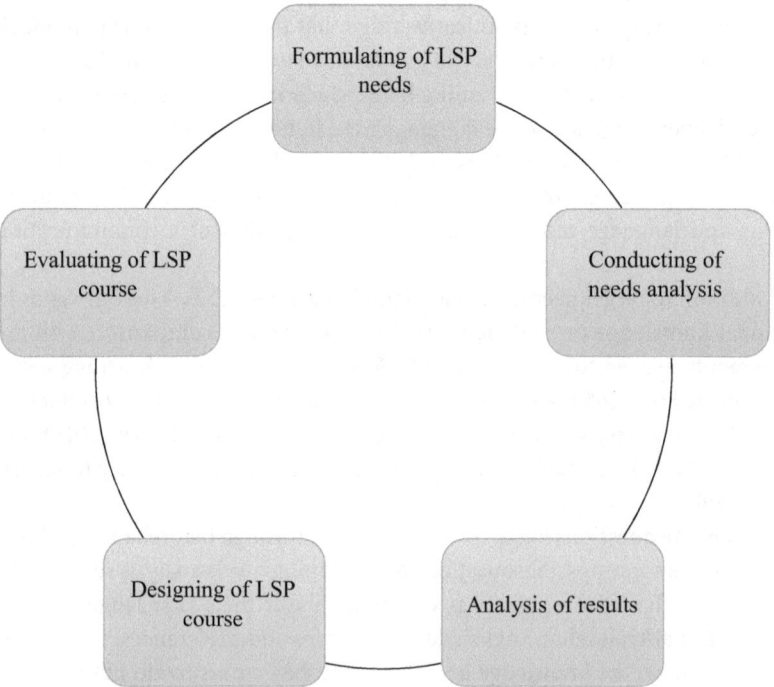

Figure 9. Cycle of needs analysis integration into a course (see Flowerdew, 2013, p. 325)

Analysing Figure 9 above, it is clear that a needs analysis should be the basis of a tailor-made specialist language course for a target group. The difference between the present and target situation may provide the basis for the syllabus, taking into consideration the learning needs. If one understands the teaching of a specialist language as the development of certain linguistic skills in professional settings, it is not possible to realise this without the necessary knowledge of those professional situations, the communicative needs those situations may evoke, and the learning needs a specific group of learners have, not to forget the potential communicative task one may have to face using LSP (target situation). The syllabus should therefore be based on data gathered from an analysis of learners' individual needs and abilities, their current situation, and the consideration of potential communicative tasks related to the target situation.

The evaluation procedure for the needs analysis should take three characteristics into account: reliability, validity, and practicality (Brown, 1989). A needs analysis is reliable only if it generates similar output when repeated after a period of time. The validity of needs analysis requires that it measures exactly what needs to be measured, while practicality is the factor comprising the financial and space costs, as well as human resources needed to conduct that evaluation (Anthony, 2018).

2.4. LSP curriculum and syllabus design

Each country has its own curriculum framework that is applied in different fields to establish a relatively standardised set of competences and skills expected to be achieved by the graduates. Thus, curricula frameworks have a key effect of the hard creative work of teachers, combining recognition of the educational circumstances, as well as identification of learner needs.

Richards (2001) defines a curriculum as a document presenting the educational process, starting from the design of its content, its implementation, and the evaluation of existing language programmes. However, this general definition does not reflect the entire complexity of curriculum design, which is the sum of many different factors.

First and foremost, this chapter will discuss factors related to curriculum creation, which include the current educational policy and cooperation with the labour market (Kic-Drgas, 2022), the current and potential needs of learners, their interests, and learning styles (Živković, 2016; Woodrow, 2018). To the above mentioned, Vos (2013) adds available resources (staff, library), programme framework and time constraints, as well as governmental directives and higher education guidelines. The factors, with their influence on the curriculum, are presented in Table 6.

Table 6. List of factors and their influence on a curriculum

Factors	Influence on the curriculum	Stability of the factor Sensitivity to changes
Current educational policy	Identification of the main sets of competences and description of particular professions including skills required.	Moderately stable; changes in legal documentation require legal procedures.
Cooperation with labour market and potential stakeholders	Real overview of the most needed skills.	Sensitive; reacting dynamically to changes on the labour market.
Scientific/academic research in the field	Analysis and identification of trends in teaching, latest reports on the use of new tools (implementation of new technology).	Moderate; changing quickly but difficult to be introduced, depending on teachers.
Available resources	Assessment of the reality of the planned undertakings considering the availability of resources.	Slow level of change; connected with financial possibilities of the institution.
Time constraints	Identification of the feasibility of the planned tasks considering the time perspective.	Very slow and unable to change.
Student needs	Identification of the expectations of students towards the course outcomes.	Sensitive; changing respectively to the situation on the labour market.

Learning is a complex process consisting of many factors, both institutional and highly individual, which have an impact on curriculum development. These factors vary in intensity and therefore also their impact can vary greatly, creating dynamic changes in the curriculum to more balanced and slower changes. Examples of changes that will affect the curriculum are the changing needs of learners, or the needs communicated by potential employers. Preparing and printing textbooks, on the other hand, is a very time-consuming process, so the pace of change will be slower.

The factors described in Table 6 and their influence on the curriculum, however, create only a very general framework for curriculum design without considering the specialisation of different fields and altering needs, as well as the results of LSP research referring to the different tools and strategies of teaching. Curriculum and syllabus development should be considered a complex task requiring not only subject but also contextual issues, such as environmental knowledge understood as the knowledge about environmental issues as well as the ability to estimate their impact on the society and further knowledge construction (Geiger et al., 2018). The development of a curriculum provides the foundation for standardised and unified learning outcomes defining what a learner will be expected to know after finishing a course, regardless of who is teaching. The curriculum should include the basic elements: goals, learning outcomes, knowledge, skills and competences, and the standards which the discussed content refers to. A curriculum also includes the description of assessment methods and materials used during a course. LSP curriculum design is a real challenge for less widely taught languages and disciplines where materials are not available and communication with stakeholders is rather limited.

There are three main types of curriculum design: the first is subject-centred design, the second is learner-centred design, and the third is problem-centred design (Basturkmen, 2010).

The first type – the subject-centred curriculum, is the most standardised form of curriculum, focused on the chosen subject. Learning needs are considered less important in the curriculum design in comparison to disciplinary knowledge. This type is used most frequently at secondary vocational schools, where LSP might be introduced as an obligatory subject and LSP teachers are supposed to cover a ministerially accepted programme.

Learner-centred curriculum design focuses on the learners first, aiming at satisfying the identified learner needs. This approach leaves free space for learners to control their learning process and co-create it. The result of implementing this design type is a tailored-made curriculum. However, adjusting the initial plans to the time restrictions and expectations of teaching institutions might be a challenge. This kind of curriculum design requires time and effort from the teacher, who needs to create materials from scratch. The learner-centred model of curriculum creation prevails in case of in-house LSP courses organised for company employees. An academic LSP course usually follows a subject-centred curriculum, whereas in-house tailor-made LSP courses organised by companies follow a learner-centred curriculum.

Problem-centred curriculum design focuses on solving real life problems that learners can be confronted with when using a foreign language. On top of that, the construction of the curriculum foresees the development of soft skills that can be applied in real life. The objectives of the curriculum should be precisely formulated, for both learners and teachers to be able to monitor progress. Also, this type of curriculum requires close cooperation with the labour market. The problem-based curriculum model is becoming more and more popular, especially in short LSP courses organised in the form of coaching for small groups or individuals with very specific needs (engineers, mathematicians, exporters, police officers).

The steps of LSP curriculum design are presented in Figure 10.

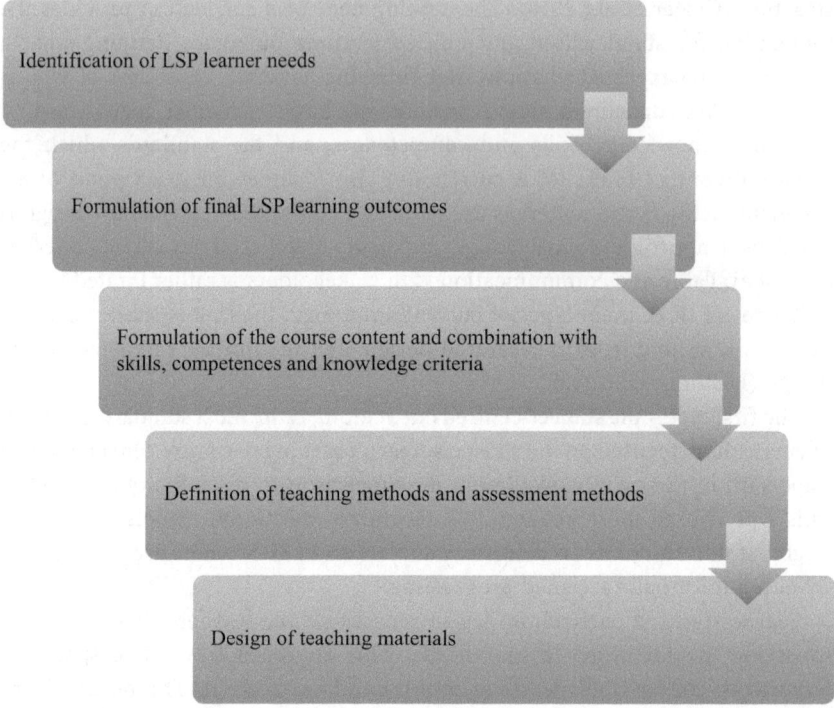

Figure 10. Steps of LSP curriculum design (see Basturkmen, 2010; Sowa, 2022a, 2022b)

The professionals designing an LSP curriculum should start with the identification of "specific language features, discourse practices and communicative skills of target groups, and adapt their teaching practices to particular subject matter and learners' expertise" (Hyland, 2002, p. 116) since an LSP curriculum needs to be in line with the methodology of the professions and disciplines it is embedded into. The identified needs form the basis for formulation of the learning outcomes, which is followed by formulation of the course content and combining it with skills, competences and knowledge categories. The next step refers to the choice of teaching methodology and assessment, which consequently lays the ground for the development of teaching materials. LSP teaching materials are developed in the course of curriculum design, and they are founded on the results of needs analysis and the LSP context. Through that they create a link between elements of the curriculum (Sierocka, 2013).

Richards (2001) underlines the necessity of correlation between the elements of the curriculum as a foundation for achieving teaching efficiency. One of the necessary aspects of LSP curriculum development differentiating it from LGP curriculum development is the goal of preparation of the learners to enter the professional world and/or completing communicational goals in a domain-specific or academic (in case of LAP or LSAP) environment. This imposes the need for constant communication with disciplinary specialists either at university level or in the professional environment.

The LSP syllabus as a sister document to the curriculum was first defined by Strevens (1977, p. 25) in the following way:

> "… partly an administrative instrument, partly a day-today guide to the teacher, partly a statement of what is to be taught and how, sometimes partly a statement of an approach. It is the document in which is listed, ideally, the items to be taught, in a particular course, to a particular set of defined learners, on a given number of occasions per week or day, in a given sequence, within the aim of achieving stated interim and final goals or objectives, and usually according to particular teaching techniques for each and every item."

Basturkmen (2010) pointed out further differences between the LSP curriculum and syllabus: a curriculum is a much broader concept which refers to the standardised tasks of the course, whereas a syllabus is a required document that communicates detailed goals, learning outcomes, etc. (Table 7).

Table 7. Differences between curriculum and syllabus (see Basturkmen, 2010)

Category	LSP curriculum	LSP syllabus
Scope	Broader concept	Narrower concept
Aim	Standards-based sequence of planned tasks and activities whose completion guarantee the achievement of proficiency in content and applied learning skills.	Communicating expectations of learners and teachers.
Content	Goals, objectives, competences and skills descriptions, standards, methods of teaching, assessment, materials.	Description of the course, course goals and objectives, students' learning outcomes, attendance policies, assessment methodology, requirements for obtaining signatures.

In the case of universities, the curriculum means all courses (number of hours, years of study, etc), while the syllabus gives details of each course. The smallest unit is the lesson plan so the hierarchy is as follows: curriculum – syllabus – lesson plan.

2.5. LSP materials design

Materials for teaching foreign languages are essential for teachers and learners. For the first of these, they provide the core for content presentation and a secure foundation for a permanent revision of the topics discussed, for the second group, the learners, materials ensure stability and are a response to the needs they have communicated. That is why the preparatory stages of materials' development should include an assessment of student target and learning needs and priorities. Since LSP is a very broad field in terms of different disciplines, and since LSP learners are very heterogeneous groups, materials which are appropriate and suitable for one LSP course may not prove so efficient for other LSP courses conducted with similar learners in similar circumstances (Marjanovikj-Apostolovski et al., 2019).

According to (Tomlinson, 1998, p. xi), materials are:

> "Anything which is used to help to teach language learners. Materials can be found in the form of a textbook, a workbook, a cassette, a CD-Rom, a video, a photocopied handout, a newspaper, a paragraph written on a whiteboard: anything which presents or informs about the language being learned."

The above definition might now be extended further as virtual objects and multimodal materials available on the Internet can be added as potential sources for LSP materials. Due to ongoing digitalisation, LSP materials have also changed their form, from stable and defined, into more virtual forms (blogs, chats, products created by AI). The Covid-19 pandemic changed attitudes and the ways of designing materials for teaching foreign languages, including LSP, breaking the established border between the tangible and abstract, between ready materials and materials undergoing co-creation in the classroom on the basis of collaboration. Alongside the current trend of digitalisation and the changes in expectations toward LSP materials, the rapid development and specialisation of many fields influencing LSP teaching (for example IT sector, AI development) should be noted. Rapid advancements also make it necessary to establish new terminology for processes and inventions that have been developed (ChatGPT, molecular farming, digital nomad, liminal space, to name just a few), which is often only manifested in the course of professional interaction. The solution for LSP teachers designing new materials is permanent access to virtual reality, where they can observe the changes in vocabulary and new terms used to name or rename concepts and processes. Also, the overweening processes of digitalisation and globalisation have contributed to the appearance of a variety of massive open online courses (MOOCs) and open educational resources (OERs) which are mainly available for free and can be easily implemented into LSP classes. All the above-mentioned tendencies are visible in the way LSP materials are currently created (see Kilickaya & Kic-Drgas, 2020; Mazzuccato & Kic-Drgas, 2021).

Krzanowski (1998) defines good, self-designed LSP materials through a set of features (Figure 11).

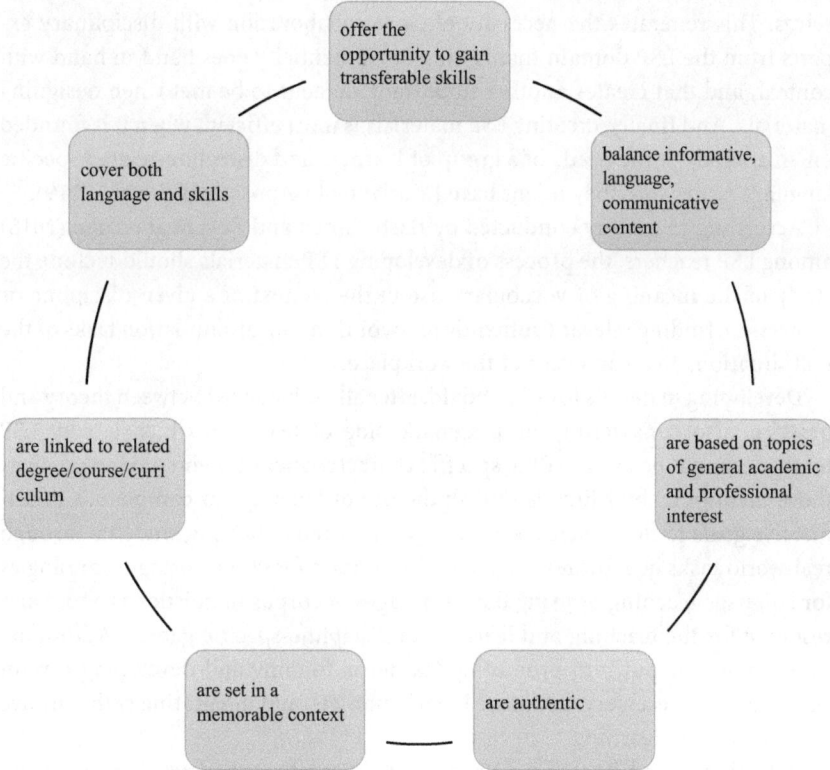

Figure 11. Features of efficient LSP materials based on Krzanowski (1998)

Krzanowski (1998) highlights the characteristics of efficient LSP teaching materials that should balance informative language and communicative content, be authentic, and set in a context that is memorable. The fulfilment of these elements facilitate the connection of specific material to the stages of the curriculum and completing the set goals, such as practising and consolidating a certain skill. Efficient LSP materials stimulate and motivate students through the creation of a real representation of register and provision of knowledge about the specialised subject area, and combine it with exposure to the syntactic and lexical elements typical for the communicative situation (Sierocka, 2013).

The elements mentioned in Figure 11 refer not only to the content but also to the skills which the use of the materials aims to develop. It is worth underlining the close relationship of teaching and learning materials to the course curriculum, syllabus, and learning outcomes designed for each LSP course. Moreover, of great importance in LSP materials design is their authenticity, which creates perhaps the biggest challenge for LSP teachers, the majority of whom are not disciplinary experts and are not directly linked to the professional world themselves. This reiterates the necessity of close collaboration with disciplinary experts from the LSP domain that is taught. Authenticity goes hand in hand with context, and that creates another important element to be met when designing materials. And finally, creating LSP materials is most efficient when it is founded on an analysis of the needs of a group of learners and discipline-related specific language issues that they might have (Marjanovikj-Apostolovskiet al., 2019).

According to a study conducted by Basturkmen and Bocanegra-Valle (2018) among LSP teachers, the process of developing LSP materials should include the study of the meaning of vocabulary use in the context of a given discipline or profession, finding relevant authentic texts, or thinking of simulation tasks of the real situations that can occur at the workplace.

Developing materials for LSP should, after all, be balanced between theory and practice, also considering the pragmatic side of teaching, which is why LSP teachers should be aware of the specific characteristics of their students, such as those mentioned by Klimova (2015): the use of language to complete communicative goals to meet their discipline-specific needs, showing students through real-world tasks how professional communication functions, using technologies for language teaching or using the advantages of corpus linguistics as a tool and resource for the teaching and learning of discipline-specific genres. Additional value should be put into promoting learner autonomy and developing certain learning skills necessary for future labour markets, and integrating collaborative and cooperative learning.

Basturkmen and Bocanegra-Valle (2018) suggest, as the first step in the development of materials, conducting thorough research of existing materials to check whether available materials are suitable to be used in the LSP course. This part of the development of materials should be in line with the assessment of learner needs. Material evaluation is a complex process, and depending "on its purpose and the context of use it can embrace different perspectives (prospective, ongoing and/or retrospective) and can be multidimensional (external and/or internal; static and/or dynamic)" (Rubdy, 2003, p. 54).

The next step after examining the available materials for LSP and the establishment of the needs of LSP learners is to either use existing materials or develop tailor-made materials for a particular LSP group of learners from scratch. Needs can be divided into present needs, target needs, and learning needs, as mentioned in the subchapter on needs analysis in LSP. The materials would thus strive to bridge the gap between the situation at present time and the requirements of the target situation, taking into consideration the learning needs of each group of LSP learners.

The adaptation of existing materials can be done following the techniques suggested by Basturkmen and Bocanegra-Valle (2018): adding, deleting, simplifying, reordering, replacing.

The biggest challenges in LSP materials design are probably the lack of available sources and the lack of contact with LSP experts from a particular domain. Sierocka (2013) also mentions the lack of self-confidence as a writer, experience and imagination, and little or no support or cooperation from staff in disciplinary departments.

Although, undeniably, developing LSP materials needs time and sometimes also financial investment, in many cases this is the only way to achieve satisfactory teaching results. Nowadays, the Internet and availability of expert websites as well as online chats can be of great benefit for LSP material designers. The introduction of AI solutions into education also creates new perspectives. In addition, creating a network with other LSP teachers, sharing their own good practices, and contacting disciplinary experts can strengthen the materials developed.

2.6. LSP teaching methodology

The aim of the subchapter is to present some teaching methods that would typically be more often used in an LSP than in an LGP classroom: task-based learning (TBL), problem-based learning (PBL), and project-based learning (PjBL).

At the very beginning, it is worth mentioning that the LSP class differs from the LGP class mainly due to the fact that in-service learners of LSP are fully aware of their needs, which might be very heterogeneous, but this may not be the case for pre-service learners, both in LGP and in LSP contexts. Apart from the natural reference to professional tasks, LSP learners are intrinsically motivated and eager to master certain linguistic skills so as to use language in a natural profession-oriented context. The principles of LSP teaching methodology are activating the links between language skills and disciplinary knowledge, and – primarily – using language in authentic-like contexts.

The first method used commonly during LSP classes is the TBL method, rooted in the communicative approach and focused on learner needs (Ellis, 2009). The TBL approach anticipates authentic communication, developing the natural use of language stimulated by the solving of tasks resembling professional situations. The LSP learner becomes an active participant and decision-maker in work-related tasks. The orientation on task accomplishment is used as the trigger for the free and natural use of foreign language. Learning comes in a more subconscious way, taking advantage of the learners' previous experience (Nunan, 2010). LSP uses innovative methods to enhance the knowledge and proper use of specific vocabulary and discourse. TBL makes learning more attractive through incorporating real-life challenges into LSP teaching and learning. TBL in LSP classes usually involves a sequence of tasks and not a single task. This sequence of tasks needs to be correlated closely and referring to the professional setting. Atabekova (2009) suggests the following stages of TBL learning (Figure 12):

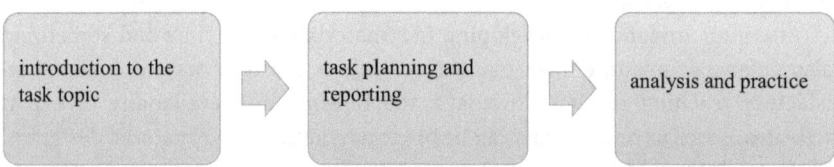

Figure 12. Stages of task-based learning (see Atabekova, 2009)

The first step relates to creating the situational background for the research, concerning the description of the task, topic or context. Then the given task is planned and reported on. In the final stage, the results are analysed and additional practice takes place.

PBL is another teaching method used in LSP classes that does not concentrate on tasks or sequences of tasks but deals with complex authentic problems that are used as stimulation to encourage student learning in a deductive way. Often, problems presented in the PBL class require the development of critical thinking and problem-solving abilities and skills, communication skills, with a strong emphasis on group work, autonomously searching for and evaluating resources, and life-long learning (Duch et al., 2001; Jurkovič, 2005). The main characteristics of PBL is work in small groups and learning by doing. The LSP teacher is more a facilitator or guide to student learning (Celinšek & Bobanović, 2022; Hmelo-Silver, 2004).

On the other hand, PjBL is a method based on the projects that learners solve using interdisciplinary knowledge and also using a foreign language naturally in a professionally oriented context. PjBL is a student-centred approach, focusing on the means of achieving the goal of completing the project. The main characteristic of the project is its context-specificity, with active involvement of the participating students and social involvement (Cocco, 2006).

Blumenfeld et al. (2000, p.150) summarise the concept of PjBL in the following way: "The presumption is that students need opportunities to construct knowledge by solving real problems through asking and refining questions, designing and conducting investigations, gathering, analysing, and interpreting information and data, drawing conclusions, and reporting findings."

PjBL prepares LSP learners for the projects they are or will be confronted with in their professional lives, which is why it is highly recommended for any kind of LSP. However, it needs to be highlighted that the preparation of a transparent and clear project description and appropriate assessment of a project requires both an interdisciplinary orientation and holistic view on evaluation from the LSP teacher. The best and most efficient way of realising PjBL in the classroom is through cooperation between the LSP teacher and a disciplinary specialist, which also applies to PBL.

The differentiation between TBL, PjBL, and PBL is not particularly clear, because all three methods share similar characteristics (student-centred and real-world problem solving). However, in PBL a specific problem is assigned to students and they need to identify the sources for solving the problem, in PjBL the problem is replaced by a complex project that requires the involvement of broader knowledge, and can be combined with the creative development of a new concept, and not only solving a problem as in PBL. PBL focuses on the product, whereas PjBL focuses on the process of project development. TBL refers to smaller communicative tasks that do not need a preparatory phase or complex research and interdisciplinary knowledge. Their aim is the development of communicative skills.

All these methods can be realised through self-directed learning, which is an approach that gives learners freedom to decide about their own development by stimulating skills development, through problem-solving life's challenges, as well as real-world projects. Learners are free to make their own learning decisions concerning the concept, content, and means of achieving set goals (Hall, 2011).

Although self-directed learning is an approach anticipating the individual work of learners, its initiation can begin in the classroom. Considering the fact that many LSP learners are adults who are either professionally active or who already have some professional experience, encouraging this way of learning might be very beneficial in the case of LSP. Self-directed learning can be introduced gradually through tasks that show learners how they can organise their own learning process (Lopes & Cunha, 2017).

2.7. LSP assessment

Dudzik et al. (2019, p. 22) provide the following definition of assessment:

> Assessment is considered an integral part of the teaching-learning process, providing key information about students' individual needs and their learning progress.

According to Chang (2014), assessment is seen as an ongoing process, which is why LSP teachers should not limit their activities only to observing students' linguistic proficiency, but they should develop tools (for example, formative assessment tests) to achieve a more complete view on students' progress. Assessment is often enlisted with evaluation and test. However, there is a significant difference in meaning between these terms.

Assessment in LSP shows how much LSP learners are equipped with LSP knowledge and skills, and how competent they are to perform well in a profession. The basic aims of LSP assessment include assigning the final grade, and preparing LSP learners for authentic communicative situations (see Anthony, 2018). Evaluation presents one's judgement on the collected data and it is usually followed by a decision-making process in order to improve the identified weaknesses. An LSP test is a tool used to check the learner's progress(see Dudzik et al., 2019).

Table 8. Purpose of assessment (see Northern Illinois University Center for Innovative Teaching and Learning (2012)[67]; Anthony, 2018)

Purpose of the assessment	Type of assessment	Purpose	Moment in the course	Instruments
Identification of needs, expectations, skills, etc.	Diagnostic	Identify strengths and weaknesses	Beginning	– Pre-test – Self-assessment – Interview
Measurement of progress	Formative	Measure degree of progress	Ongoing	– Observation of in-class activities – Reflection journal – Q&A session – Homework – In-class activity – Student feedback collected by periodically answering specific questions

---

[67] Northern Illinois University Center for Innovative Teaching and Learning. (2012). Formative and summative assessment. In Instructional guide for university faculty and teaching assistants. Retrieved from https://www.niu.edu/citl/resources/guides/instructional-guide.

Table 8 *(Continued)*

Purpose of the assessment	Type of assessment	Purpose	Moment in the course	Instruments
Evaluation of progress	Summative	Assess the adequacy of progress	End	- Project - Portfolio - Examination - Final examination - Term paper - Instructor self-evaluation - Student evaluation of the course

Table 8 shows the differences between diagnostic, formative, and summative assessment. Diagnostic assessment provides feedback on the current state of knowledge, usually before the start of the course. Formative assessment provides continuous feedback during the course, measuring students' progress and identifying the potential fields of improvement, as such is more process-oriented. Summative assessment is, in turn, a product-oriented assessment occurring at the end of some period to check the efficiency of teaching.

Tests as instruments for gathering information on students' language abilities should be characterised, among others, by the following qualities (Bachman and Palmer, 1996, pp. 17–42):
- reliability – means that a test produces consistent results if repeated.
- validity – means the accuracy with which a test measures what it is supposed to measure. According to Puppin (2007), reliable and valid tests are likely to produce positive feedback, but if the test does not cover the specific material taught in the classroom, the students will find the testing experience stressful and the results will not reflect the level of students' ability.
- authenticity – refers to the correlation between the tasks of the test on the one hand, and language use in authentic, target language situations on the other. Authenticity can be treated as essential for content validity and reliability in LSP tests which claim to "serve as an assessment tool in the real world" (Wu & Stansfield, 2001, p. 187).
- interactiveness – means the involvement of an individual in completing a certain task. According to Bachman and Palmer (1996, pp. 28–29), both authenticity and interactiveness are relative and the minimum acceptable levels specified for authenticity and interactiveness depend on the requirements of a given testing situation.

- practicality – refers to the economy of time, effort and resources in testing, or how easy it is to design, construct and interpret test results.

Dudzik et al. (2019) highlight the following characteristics of LSP tests, differentiating them from LGP tests: specialist knowledge and professional context. Following Omaggio's (1986) suggestion, LSP tests should address potential communicative situations in the professional context.

In LSP assessment, achievement and proficiency tests can overlap. If the course prepares the students to deal with the use of knowledge that they have acquired in real-life situations, the aim and scope of both tests are the same.

2.8. Synthesis

In this chapter, we have pointed out the essential elements concerning LSP teaching, taking into account the most recent literature on the subject. As a prelude to this discussion, we have chosen "an approach to language learning, which is based on learner need." (Hutchinson & Waters, 1987, p. 19) and its extension, "the teaching and research of language in relation to the communicative needs of speakers of a second language in facing a particular workplace, academic, or professional context" (Basturkmen & Elder, 2004, p. 672). However, it is always worth emphasising the importance of each particular field of study, which greatly influences the character and form of specialised language.

The division of this chapter was loosely dictated by Anthony's identification of the four pillars of LSP teaching: needs analysis, learning objectives, materials and methods, and evaluation (Anthony, 2018).

Particular attention has been given to the scope, types and interpretation of needs analysis as a determinant of the effectiveness of the LSP teaching process. The crucial role of needs is reflected in the fact that it is not possible to realise an LSP course without the necessary knowledge of those professional situations, the communicative needs those situations may evoke, and the learning needs a specific group of LSP learners has.

All these things together become an invaluable aid in the preparation of curricula and syllabuses for LSP. Following Basturkmen (2010), three main categories of curriculum design are elucidated: subject-centred, learner-centred, and problem-centred design. However, an academic LSP course usually follows a subject-centred curriculum, whereas in-house tailor-made LSP courses organised by companies follow a learner-centred curriculum. There are several factors influencing curriculum design, such as current educational policy, cooperation with labour markets and potential stakeholders, scientific research findings, available resources, time constraints, and student needs.

The next subchapter aims at outlining the development of LSP materials as one of the biggest challenges that LSP teachers need to deal with before, during, and after the LSP teaching process (Petraki & Khat, 2020), not only due to their limited availability (especially in the case of less widespread LSPs) but also due to their slow rate of adaptiveness to the developments in the labour market and in respect of the needs that each specific group of LSP learners has.

Concerning the teaching methodology of the LSP class, characteristic methods are PjBL, TBL, and PBL. All three are very similar to each other, but also inherently different, and their effectiveness in LSP teaching is due to their high degree of leeway, interdisciplinarity, and learner space. If in PjBL the tasks are designed to be project-based, in TBL they are task-specific. PBL focuses on the product, whereas PjBL focuses on the process of project development. TBL refers to smaller communicative tasks that do not need a preparatory phase, or complex research and interdisciplinary knowledge. The last part of the chapter is devoted to the specifics of LSP assessment, which differs from general language assessment mainly due to the context and situational relevance of the communicative skills of the linguistic activity in question. LSP test features are also thematised as instruments for gathering information on students' language abilities (Bachman & Palmer, 1996), incorporating abilities such as reliability, validity, authenticity, instructiveness, practicality and, in the case of LSP tests, also disciplinary knowledge and professional context.

3. LSP teachers

3.1. Introduction

Already in 1997, Richards stated that "surprisingly little is known about the professional lives and beliefs of ESP teachers around the world." (p. 51), which is – despite the growing attention dedicated to LSP in recent years – at least in part also true also today. In fact, we may agree with Belcher (2013) who claims that the LSP community undoubtedly has broad knowledge in many aspects related to LSP but at the same time knows least about their own professional community.

In an attempt to compensate for the insufficient attention dedicated to LSP teachers, this chapter addresses the multifaceted roles, competences, identities, and challenges that they assume throughout their teaching careers. It therefore focuses on various dimensions of LSP teachers, shedding light on the critical elements that contribute to effective language instruction. It first discusses the diverse roles that LSP teachers undertake in their classrooms, and continues by outlining the competences required for successful LSP teaching. The significance of LSP teachers' understanding of both the target language and the specific disciplinary content is highlighted in the following subchapter. This subchapter also explores how LSP teachers bridge the gap between language learning and disciplinary knowledge, facilitating students' ability to communicate effectively in their chosen discipline. This is followed by a brief discussion of the notion of LSP teacher identity. It examines the self-perception of LSP teachers in relation to their roles, competences, and the broader educational community. Highlighting the obstacles that LSP teachers often encounter, the chapter continues with the identification and discussion of various challenges of LSP teachers, such as integrating authentic disciplinary materials, adapting to changing technological landscapes, and managing diverse student needs. Concluding the chapter, the concept of LSP communities of practice is explored, highlighting in particular the importance of collaborative networks for LSP teachers to share experiences, insights, and best practices.

3.2. LSP teacher roles

There is a certain degree of overlap between the roles that LGP and LSP teachers need to play in their classrooms to create the conditions for effective language teaching and learning, for instance the roles of classroom manager, teacher of the language skills, and encourager of learner autonomy, to mention just a few (Jurkovič et al., 2023). In other words, some of the roles that an LSP teacher undertakes are aligned with the roles played by an LGP teacher. This section will mainly focus on those roles of LSP teachers that stem from the specificities of LSP teaching compared to LGP teaching. In fact, it may be assumed that LSP differs from LGP in particular in terms of the additional roles, engendered by the specific nature of LSP, that LSP teachers need to undertake (Nazari, 2020) and thus new functions, tasks, and expectations that LSP teachers need to meet (Przybył, 2022).

LSP teachers may assume a wide inventory of roles (Paltridge, 2013). Traditionally speaking, these include the roles of (Dudley-Evans & StJohn, 1998):
- classroom teacher (e.g., teaching the language skills and terminology),
- course designer (e.g., defining the content and methodology of an LSP course),
- materials provider (e.g., choosing, adapting, or writing teaching and learning materials),
- collaborator (e.g., collaborating with peers, disciplinary specialists, and learners),
- researcher (e.g., researching language use in the target discipline), and
- evaluator (e.g., evaluating learners, courses, class materials, and teaching and learning methodology).

If the four pillars of LSP as defined by Anthony (2018) are taken into consideration – needs analysis, learning objectives, materials design and methodology, and evaluation – then a key role that LSP teachers play also is that of needs analyst (of academic and/or occupational needs, target needs, learning needs, etc.). In terms of the role of provider of disciplinary knowledge, the extent to which LSP teachers need to master the discipline that their LSP is embedded into still is an issue under debate and is referred to in various sections of this book. Nevertheless, it should be mentioned that in most cases the students, especially those in advanced years of academic study, will have a better knowledge of the discipline than their LSP teachers (Dudley-Evans & StJohn, 1998). This means that their roles in the classroom can often become inverted so that the students become their LSP teacher's teachers in a joint and bilateral process of knowledge construction (Słocińska, 2013). In this case, the LSP teacher may assume the role of learner and learn from their students (Medrea & Rus, 2012).

The developments in the specific fields of linguistics, applied linguistics, language teaching methodology, and the broader field of digital technologies used in teaching have expanded and altered the roles of LSP teachers, too. These new roles can be seen as integral parts of the traditional roles described above. The first example derives from the use of data-driven learning. If language corpora are used in the teaching and learning process, the LSP teachers will assume the role of guides and facilitators instead of the traditional roles of input providers (in this case input is provided by the data) and instructors (Chen et al., 2019). Moreover, we are witnessing increasing awareness that language learning is not limited to and/or does not cease outside language classrooms but can instead exploit the almost never-ending opportunities for informal learning, in particular in online contexts (Jurkovič, 2019). Consequently, LSP teachers (but also LGP teachers, of course) have also become lifelong learning mentors (Bocanegra-Valle, 2012). Next, numerous classes worldwide are less and less homogeneous in terms of the first language of the learners. This implies a new role of LSP teachers as cultural mediators (Bocanegra-Valle, 2012), in which intercultural communication and interaction is not only seen as communication between and among national cultures but also as communication between and among disciplines (Spencer-Oatey & Franklin, 2009). Last but not least, during and after the Covid-19 pandemic years, the need for self-regulated and autonomous learning tremendously increased. This, however, did not diminish the role of teachers. The process that they underwent was that of continuous adaptation and re-evaluation of their teaching practices, classroom materials, and assessment forms, which allowed them to meet the conditions engendered by a situation that they had never experienced before.

A comprehensive contemporary and research-based analysis of LSP teacher roles was provided by Vega Umaña (2020). Her study conducted among higher education LSP teachers in France showed that the roles that LSP teachers undertake may be divided into three broad categories. These are: domains of action, domains of expertise, and interactional and relational roles.

First, the main role that LSP teachers assume within the domains of action is that of knowledge providers, facilitators and guides that primarily address learners' professional and general needs. Next, LSP teachers' roles within their domains of expertise include those of language experts, disciplinary experts, cultural experts, and language teaching methodology experts. Finally, the interactional and relational roles see LSP teachers as learners but also as providers of psychological and emotional support.

3.3. LSP teacher competences

The competences, understood as "a combination of knowledge, skills and attitudes appropriate to the context" (European Commission, 2018, p.1) that LSP teachers need to have to be able to teach efficiently are closely related to the diversity of roles that they will play within the process of LSP teaching and learning (Sowa, 2022b), and that have been described in the previous pages. Nevertheless, still not much is known about the specific knowledge, skills, and competences that LSP teachers are required to have, and how these skills and competences are developed (Bocanegra-Valle & Basturkmen, 2019).

If based on Anthony's (2018) four pillars of LSP, an LSP teacher needs to have competences in particular in the fields of needs analysis, definition of learning objectives within syllabus design, materials design and methodology, and evaluation. These have been covered in the previous chapter in this book. A literature review, however, indicated some areas of LSP teacher competences that partially but not entirely overlap with these pillars. These are discipline-specific, language analytic, and transferable competences that undoubtedly can be defined as belonging to core LSP teacher competences.

First, the question whether LSP teachers need to master the discipline that their LSP is embedded in still is a controversial issue. While numerous LSP teachers may feel that disciplinary knowledge is not essential for linguists (Van der Yeught, 2016), most researchers nowadays seem to agree that disciplinary acculturation or acquisition of a sufficient amount of knowledge of the discipline (Chen, 2000) contributes to the LSP teachers' credibility and confidence (Jurkovič et al., 2023; Podgoršek et al., 2021). In other words, lack of disciplinary knowledge may result in feelings of anxiety and stress, which will in turn negatively affect the classroom atmosphere (Iswati & Triastuti, 2021). From the learners' perspective, learners will find courses that are more specifically tailored to their disciplines more useful (Kennedy & Bolitho, 1984). In addition, an LSP teacher that has a fair understanding of the disciplinary context will be able to engage in better professional communication with their students (Dudley-Evans & StJohn, 1998). Therefore, the general language proficiency is not enough and must be supported by disciplinary knowledge (Maleki, 2008) that usually exceeds the common knowledge of educated native speakers in that particular domain (Tudor, 1997). Interestingly, the findings of Vega Umaña (2020) indicated that the majority of French higher education LSP teachers feel comfortable with their disciplinary knowledge, the types of genres that their learners should be prepared to understand and produce, and discipline-specific terminology. Within the community of Maritime English teachers, this debate has resulted in the dilemma whether the positions of Maritime English teachers should actually be taken by LSP teachers with a linguistic background that have become *marinated* and have thus acquired sufficient disciplinary credibility, or former seafarers with extensive disciplinary knowledge that have become skilled in language teaching (Cole et al., 2007). However, the assumption that LSP teachers need to have a degree of disciplinary knowledge leads to the question where and how this knowledge can be developed. Several possible resources can be found in a dedicated subchapter on LSP disciplinary knowledge and knowledge of language use in the context.

Next, in order to efficiently perform the role of researcher of language use in the target discipline, which will in turn translate into tailor-made and learner-centred teaching and learning materials, an LSP teacher needs to be a confident language analyst with analytical competences. Therefore, the genre and discourse analytical competence is of crucial importance for LSP teachers (Jarvis, 1983). Language analysis entails LSP discourse awareness, discourse analysis skills, basic knowledge in corpus linguistics, and at least basic knowledge in quantitative and qualitative research methodology (Turula & Gajewska, 2019). In fact, only an LSP teacher that has the competence to analyse specialised text and discourse can efficiently define the learning objectives and in turn design course materials and language activities that will enable the achievement of these objectives (Tudor, 1997). Dudley-Evans (2001) took this statement a step further in claiming that LSP teachers must in fact become *genre doctors*. The ability to analyse discipline-specific genres with their linguistic peculiarities will enable LSP teachers to adapt also to unpredictable teaching situations (Hüttner et al., 2009). As mentioned, language analysis as a part of the broader framework of needs analysis is of utmost importance for course, syllabus, and materials design. A particular challenge for LSP teachers is to master this process in a discipline that is not their own (Tudor, 1997).

Among the soft or transferable skills, a key quality that an LSP teacher may possess is flexibility (Robinson, 1991). This is related to adaptability or the competence of LSP teachers to deal with the unpredictability of the situations that they (will) meet in their professional lives, that stem from the different LSP domains, and different LSPs that they might be required to teach (Hüttner et al., 2009). Undoubtedly, a very important competence is the learning of how to learn, acquire new knowledge, skills, and competences, and thus adapt to the developing circumstances engendered by disciplinary developments. Recently, the number of homogeneous classes by the first language of the learners has been decreasing. This corroborates the importance of another key transferable competence, which is the intercultural competence (Spencer-Oatey & Franklin, 2009; Tudor, 1997; Turula & Gajewska, 2019; Vega Umaña, 2020), necessary to efficiently play the role of cultural mediators, as mentioned in the previous subchapter.

A comprehensive research study into the professional development needs of LSP teachers conducted by Jurkovič et al. (2023) also showed the need for a clear competence framework for LSP teachers that would enable their community to clearly define the roles that they would need to undertake and the competences that they would be required to develop. This competence framework could be based on the related Competency Framework for Teachers of English for Academic Purposes developed by the British Association of Lecturers in English for Academic Purposes (BALEAP, 2008). BALEAP's competence framework is divided into four domains: academic practice, EAP students, curriculum development, and programme implementation. These are first described with a summary of competence statements. Some examples are provided below (BALEAP, 2008, p. 3):

- Academic practice: "An EAP teacher will be able to recognise and explore disciplinary differences and how they influence the way knowledge is expanded and communicated."
- EAP students: "An EAP teacher will understand the requirements of the target context that students wish to enter …"
- Curriculum development: "An EAP teacher will understand approaches to text classification and discourse analysis …"
- Programme implementation: "An EAP teacher will be able to assess academic language and skills tasks using formative and summative assessment."

These domains of competence clearly reveal the interrelatedness between the worlds of EAP and LSP but also a significant difference. In fact, EAP teachers would usually not be expected to conduct target needs analysis (except in contexts where EAP or another language for academic purposes is taught in specific contexts as an LSAP), with the exception of present situational analysis and learning needs analysis. This further corroborates the need for a dedicated competency framework for LSP teachers based on areas of LSP teacher competence identified in the literature, and the LSP Teacher Common Competence Framework[68], developed as one of the results of the Catapult project.

---

[68] http://catapult-project.eu/wp-content/uploads/2019/11/CATAPULT_LSP_Teacher_CCF_v12.pdf.

3.4. LSP teachers' knowledge of the discipline and knowledge of language use in context

LSP teaching relates to language knowledge but also includes discipline-specific knowledge that relates to a certain domain. This subchapter includes a brief overview of the definitions and uses of LSP disciplinary knowledge, and knowledge of language use in the disciplinary context.

Douglas (2000, p. 2) reflects, analysing the differences and similarities between LSP and LGP, that the element that distinguishes both the above is the "interaction between language knowledge and specific purpose content knowledge". An LSP is combined with a specific domain, such as medicine, economics, or technology, which results in the need for specific knowledge, enabling us to recognise and name the given professional reality. The ability to create statements or texts related to a specific fragment of professional reality implies the presence of the relevant knowledge in the minds of potential communicative partners. However, it is important to underline that that knowledge is the result of an individual process of construction, resulting from individual experience, research and beliefs, which means nobody can simply share knowledge with anybody else, but merely present a certain content in order to stimulate a certain reaction (including knowledge construction). Therefore, specialised knowledge is generated as a result of specific language operations (Bajerowska, 2013; Grucza, 2013).

The complexity of LSP teaching requires a distinction between specialist linguistic knowledge, methodological preparation, and disciplinary or specialist professional knowledge (see Sowa, 2016, 2022a).

Specialist linguistic knowledge refers, on the one hand, to proficiency in language skills, and on the other to the ability of text analysis (especially discipline-specific texts) enabling the identification of the most salient properties of given genres. Basic knowledge of discourse and genre analysis may be useful, for example, in designing learning materials. Since language does not function in isolation, part of specialist linguistic knowledge is also the ability to comprehend and contrastively present the similarities and differences between L1 and L2. In short, specialist linguistic knowledge refers to the meta-linguistic knowledge about the functioning of language.

Methodological preparation refers to collecting information about the learning needs of each student group, their analysis, preparation of adequate teaching materials and implementation of efficient teaching methods by introducing material in class. In the case of LSP other than economics or law, the choice of teaching materials is very limited (Kic-Drgas & Woźniak, 2022a). In short, methodological preparation involves knowledge of how linguistic material should be taught.

Specialist professional knowledge, which is understood as disciplinary knowledge or knowledge about a particular domain (for example, how economics function, or how legal acts are adopted), allows us to understand the terms used in specific discourse, concepts and processes that these terms verbalise, which consequently enables efficient communication in professional contexts.

The question, however, of how much disciplinary knowledge an LSP teacher requires may thus be a question that is context-dependent. Berdychowska (2010, p. 64) points out that for an LSP teacher knowledge has two dimensions: linguistic but also practical, i.e., "the ability to recognise and use linguistic indicators of specialist texts and reconstruct the structure of a fragment of knowledge represented in specific texts and to express specialist knowledge of the above-mentioned ranges in texts."

This last type of knowledge raises numerous controversies, since LSP teachers usually are not experts in the specific disciplines, as is mentioned in several subchapters of this book. Early (1981, p. 81) points out the asymmetry of knowledge between LSP teachers and LSP learners:

> It is true that he or she possesses specialist knowledge of the target language which the learner is interested in acquiring; he or she may be fortunate enough to possess some familiarity with the subject matter relevant to the learner's area of study or concentration. It is more likely, however (…) that the learner will possess far more knowledge in depth in his or her own specialist field than the teacher.

The statement above goes in line with the stimulation of knowledge construction presented by Słocińska (2013) who distinguishes between:
- Unilateral flow – meaning the asymmetric roles of communication partners, which can be compared to an LGP class in which the teacher presenting linguistic knowledge presents it and motivates the behaviour of students.
- Bilateral flow – meaning the symmetric roles of communication partners, which can be compared to LSP, in which both the teacher presenting linguistic knowledge and learner presenting disciplinary knowledge can mutually motivate each other.

Although LSP teachers do not have to be experts in the particular domain, the development of disciplinary knowledge remains one of the greatest challenges for LSP teachers (Bocanegra-Valle & Basturkmen, 2019). Therefore, awareness of the context of the discipline is one of the basic knowledge-related needs of LSP teachers (Bocanegra-Valle and Perea-Barbera, 2023; Jurkovič et al., 2023).

One of the teacher's essential competences in relation to knowledge and its construction is the ability to search for and select new information related to the subject independently, and to learn autonomously. Below, some suggestions for self-regulated development of disciplinary knowledge for LSP teachers are presented.

Available textbooks, mainly content-related, can be an important starting point for further analysis. Books describing LSP teacher education and professional development are still scarce (Woodrow, 2018; Anthony, 2018) and mainly limited to ESP. An important source of information can be either LSP textbooks for a particular domain or textbooks for that particular domain (e.g, Transport Law) designed for students to learn about the discipline.

Courses offered by certain institutions (e.g., chambers of commerce) and examinations to certify these competences can be also very helpful. These include, for example, the Further Certificate for Teachers of Business English (FTBE) or the *Diplôme de Didactique en Français sur Objectifs Spécifiques* (DDiFOS). The tests check the knowledge of Business English methodology and textbooks, ability to design an LSP course, and so on, and knowledge of terminology in various fields of business, as well as business correspondence. It should be emphasised that such courses exist only for larger and more popular languages and disciplines (Gajewska & Sowa, 2015).

In-house mentoring of more experienced colleagues is an essential part of gaining knowledge for novice teachers first starting their professional careers (Jurkovič et al., 2023). In-house support and tutoring are efficient ways to solve initial difficulties on the spot and also to observe good practices.

Close cooperation with disciplinary teachers (including attending their courses) is an important element to enhance LSP teachers' specialist professional knowledge. This is not only about the exchange of experiences, but also about the realisation of joint projects which are important for both sides and therefore activate students to use both linguistic and disciplinary knowledge. An example of such cooperation is the CLILig project carried out by Poznan University of Technology[69], in which a project group from automation and robotics examined the comfort of living in an intelligent house and, using a self-constructed model, explained the principle of operation of an intelligent building. All project communication and the final presentation were conducted in a foreign language, which was possible thanks to the involvement of both disciplinary experts and qualified LSP teachers (Gajewska & Sowa, 2015; Gajewska et al., 2020; Kic-Drgas, 2022).

Literature and papers from the given discipline are also important and can be a valuable guide to changing specific terminology. Another relevant resource for

---

69 https://www.clc.put.poznan.pl/uni-clilig.

up-to-date terminology can be genre analysis of authentic documents and the creation of word and reference lists of the most frequently used words and terms through the application of corpus analysis tools.

An important source of knowledge can also be YouTube, or audio-visual materials available on the Internet that often explain specific content in an easy way.

Finally, conferences on the teaching of specialised languages or conferences in the discipline, and papers published in scientific and methodological journals on language as well as in the related discipline, are an important source to stimulate the development of disciplinary knowledge.

3.5. LSP teacher identity

Language teacher identity can be described as how language teachers perceive themselves and how they think they are perceived by others, and how they see themselves in relation to the work that they do (Barkhuizen, 2021). Importantly, teacher identity is not a fixed state. Instead, it is variable and subject to development as a result of the daily activities (Wenger, 1998) that teachers perform within their teaching and professional contexts. This in turn means that teacher identity largely derives from the roles that they play in the LSP classroom, and the broader LSP community. As their roles might change and develop through their teaching careers, so can their teacher identity.

Understanding the complex identities that foreign language teachers construct is crucial (Kayi-Aydar, 2019; Pennington, 2015) also because their identities serve as the foundation for classroom work, and growth, both personal and professional (Yaza & Lindahl, 2020). In addition, "to understand language teaching and learning, we need to understand teachers: the professional, cultural, political, and individual identities which they claim or which are assigned to them" (Varghese et al., 2005, p. 22). By analogy, if we want to understand LSP teaching, we first need to understand LSP teachers and their identity.

The complex nature of LSP teacher professional identity was described by Chang (2017) who recognised eight key professional identities for LSP teachers. They are shown in Figure 13.

On the other hand, an influential model of contextual frames that can be used to represent different aspects of teacher identity in the field of Teaching English to Speakers of Other Languages (TESOL) was developed by Pennington (2015). Taken as a whole, the contextual frames constitute the complex identity of TESOL teachers and conceptualise what it means to be one. Pennington's (2015) model was applied in a research study of teacher identity for ESP teachers by Mahendra (2020), aiming to explore teacher identity in ESP teaching and learning

Figure 13. Key professional identities of LSP teachers (Chang, 2017)

among four ESP teachers in a language institute. Table 9 merges Pennington's (2015) definitions of the five practice-centred frames of teacher identity, and Mahendra's (2020) findings for ESP teachers in an attempt to provide a clear and comprehensive overview of LSP teacher identity based on these two resources.

Table 9. LSP teacher identity (Mahendra, 2020) based on the practice-centred frames of teacher identity (Pennington, 2015)

Frame	Description (Pennington, 2015)	ESP teacher identity (Mahedra, 2020)
Instructional	– The content and methods of instruction, including how a teacher conceptualises and performs teaching. – Definition of the teacher in the classroom and their roles. – Teacher–student relationship that the teacher establishes.	– Importance of acquiring knowledge of the discipline. – Complexity of LSP compared with LGP. – Need for collaboration between teachers and learners. – Importance of previous professional experience, also with work in the industry.
Discipline-related	– Connection between the teacher and specific areas of knowledge and research (e.g., linguistics, applied linguistics, education, and psychology).	– Identification with the discipline. – Influence of contextual factors on the status of LSP. – Awareness of the fluid importance of LSP in each context.

Table 9 (Continued)

Frame	Description (Pennington, 2015)	ESP teacher identity (Mahedra, 2020)
Professional	- Variation and adaptation to the context within the framework set by the standards and practices. - Connection between the teacher and professional bodies (e.g., associations).	- Internalisation of the need for constant development of knowledge of the discipline. - Internalisation of the need for engagement in the professional community. - Development of the awareness of the importance of professional growth.
Vocational	- The affective component related to the commitment to teaching in a specific field or context. - The affective component related to the commitment to the learners.	- Positive attitude toward LSP based on its perceived benefits. - Contribution of LSP teaching to a sense of fulfilment as a teacher. - Importance of continuous professional development. - Internalisation of the perception of self as a lifelong learner. - Feeling of enjoyment when designing materials or evaluating.
Economic	- Considerations with an impact on a teacher's level of satisfaction. - The extent and success of participation in academic contexts (e.g., publication of papers), which help create a teacher's "academic capital". This can contribute to the teacher's satisfaction and positive self-image, position, and economic compensation.	- Students' superior socio-economic status. - Construction of teacher identity through the acquisition of knowledge of the discipline within the professional community.

Mahendra's (2020) results indicate several important factors that contribute to the development of an LSP teacher's identity. The first seems to be the importance of the acquisition or further development of disciplinary knowledge through a collaboration process with the learners and/or colleagues, engagement in the professional community, and self-learning. Similar findings were proposed by Tao and Gao (2018), namely that LSP teachers construct their identity through the acquisition of disciplinary knowledge and engagement with professional communities. Professional development also allows LSP teachers to reconstruct their knowledge inventory, and acquire new disciplinary knowledge and skills, which in turn has a positive effect on their teacher identity, self-image, and confidence (Li, 2022).

Another important factor is the importance of the context of LSP teaching. If the need for LSP knowledge and skills in a given environment is high, this may have a beneficial effect on the status of the LSP teacher, a sense of fulfilment as a teacher, and hence on a positive development of the LSP teacher identity. It seems that the ESP teachers involved in Mahendra's study (2020) developed a feeling of identification with the discipline, also because of the perceived benefits that LSP teaching has for their learners, which was also found by Tao and Gao (2018). Last but not least, the often intrinsic need for life-long professional development calls for opportunities and incentives for LSP teachers to engage in LSP research and professional development events.

A controversial aspect of LSP teacher identity is linked to the economic frame. In fact, Mahendra (2020) found that the socio-economic status of the learners may be higher than that of their LSP teachers. In relation to this, Tao and Gao (2018) advise the establishment of a system of incentives that would reward the LSP teachers for the additional time and effort that they invest into their teaching and professional development.

English is the most widely taught LSP (Jurkovič et al., 2023) while other LSPs seem to play a more marginal role. Importantly, the LSP teacher identity also is related to the contextual factors and the perceived relevance of LSP teaching in the broader environment (Mahendra, 2020). Therefore, it may be assumed that the identity of ESP teachers would be different from the identity of teachers of other LSPs, which is a research gap that further studies may attempt to bridge. This is in line with Anesa's and Deyrich's (2022) thoughts that the language and related culture is one of the four main aspects (in addition to discipline, institution, and school of thought) that determine an LSP teacher's multidimensional identity. Although the number of studies into ESP teacher identity has been increasing, the identity of teachers of LSPs other than English but also ESP remains an under-researched topic (Chang, 2017). In fact, also the status of LSP and ESP teachers and teaching which – as presented above – exerts an influence on the development of LSP teacher identity, has been a long-standing issue throughout the world. Already Hutchinson and Waters (1987) described the nature of LSP as being in the service of other disciplines, thus acknowledging its somehow subordinate role. This may negatively impact the collaboration between disciplinary and LSP teachers that is also often related to the (perceived) lower status of LSP teachers compared to faculty staff in the specific discipline (Stewart, 2018).

3.6. LSP teacher challenges

The complexity and specificity of LSP teachers' roles, of the competences that LSP teachers are required to have to build opportunities for efficient LSP teaching and learning, the lack of suitable pre-service and in-service professional development programmes, and the ensuing changeable and developing nature of LSP teacher identity – each of these aspects has been discussed in the previous subchapter – result in a series of challenges that LSP teachers need to cope with at various stages of their teaching careers.

As early as 1983, Ewer provided a classification of five groups of difficulties – in other words, challenges – that foreign language teachers experience when transitioning from the teaching of LGP to the teaching of LSP. These groups are:
- attitudinal difficulties (stemming from the LSP teacher's attitude to the discipline),
- conceptual (stemming from the need to acquire an outline knowledge of the discipline),
- linguistic (stemming from the specific language used to conceptualise the disciplinary knowledge),
- methodological (stemming from the type and age of students, as well as teaching methodologies typical of the related discipline), and
- organisational (stemming from administrative requirements).

Four decades later, a framework of challenges experienced by LSP teachers was constructed by Iswati and Triastuti (2021).

The first challenge stems from insufficient disciplinary knowledge (Iswati & Triastuti, 2021). This means that, at least at the beginning of their teaching careers, LSP teachers will most probably be unfamiliar with the disciplinary context (Alsharif & Shukri, 2018). The lack of disciplinary knowledge may lead to embarrassment, huge time investments into class preparation (Duyen, 2014), anxiety and stress (Iswati & Triastuti, 2021), and lack of self-confidence (Podgoršek et al., 2021). A potential solution to this challenge might lie in in-house mentoring by more experienced LSP teachers (Jurkovič et al., 2023) where this is possible. If the LSP teacher is the only LSP teacher at an institution and therefore works in isolation, they will have to rely on their self-direction skills for professional self-development that will allow them to explore the disciplinary context individually (Almabekova, 2010) through self-study, attendance at conferences, observations of the disciplinary specialists' classes, and so on. Last but not least, what is important in LSP teaching is the cooperation with the disciplinary specialists at various stages of the teaching process (Iswati & Triastuti, 2021), for instance when selecting or designing teaching materials. In this way, the problems related to the LSP teacher's lack of disciplinary knowledge can be reduced (Alsharif & Shukri, 2018).

The second challenge refers to the lack of pre-service education and in-service professional development (Iswati & Triastuti, 2021), discussed in several subchapters of this book. Here let us only restate that possible solutions to this challenge might be provided by online self-regulated courses for LSP teachers developed within the Catapult (http://catapult-project.eu/) and LSP-TEOC.Pro (https://lsp-teoc-pro.de/) projects. These, however, are aimed at LSP teachers from different fields and therefore need to be supplemented by self-development (Ali, 2015) and/or in-house mentoring (Jurkovič et al., 2023), as mentioned above, especially for LSP teachers from niche disciplines and of LSPs other than English, for whom relevant and personalised professional development opportunities are scarcer.

The third challenge identified by Iswati and Triastuti (2021) originates from the lack of proper needs analysis, which means that the syllabus and teaching materials are not built on data gathered among relevant stakeholders. This may be a result of the lack of familiarity with suitable needs analysis tools (Sowa, 2022b). Challenges related to needs analysis, yet from a slightly different perspective, were also identified by Anthony (2018) who states that the learners might not have a full awareness of their learning and target needs, and that LSP teachers might have their own necessities, lacks, and wants for an LSP course. Moreover, the absence of the results of a proper needs analysis may result in unspecified, unclear, lacking detail, or even wrong course objectives (Anthony, 2018). This will in turn create challenges in designing relevant materials, choosing adequate teaching methods, and defining appropriate evaluation and assessment instruments and techniques.

Iswati's and Triastuti's (2021) fourth and fifth challenges refer to what Duyen (2014) classified under objective challenges. These include large class sizes and learners' varied pre-existing abilities in the foreign language, which was also found in other contexts (e.g., Podgoršek et al., 2021). As a potential solution, Duyen (2014) suggests a division of LSP courses into compulsory and optional elements. For example, this approach was adopted in the teaching of Maritime English, where the International Maritime Organization (2015) suggests an optional General Maritime English course at the elementary to intermediate levels for students who need to build the required knowledge base, and compulsory specific courses at the upper-intermediate level for all students in the maritime domain.

In addition to the challenges identified by Iswati and Triastuti (2021), Anthony (2018) and Podgoršek et al. (2021) highlight challenges related to LSP materials and methods, in particular those associated with locating suitable materials, and dealing with disciplinary vocabulary. In this respect, Hüttner et al.

(2009) suggest that empowering pre-service (but also in-service) LSP teachers for the autonomous analysis of genres that are typical of a specific discipline appears as essential. This will allow them to locate the most important genres that the LSP materials can be based on, and analyse the disciplinary vocabulary that they contain.

Last but not least, although cooperation with disciplinary specialists was identified as a possible solution to some of the challenges presented above, it may itself become a significant challenge (Anthony, 2018; Podgoršek et al., 2021). In fact, the status of LSP teachers compared to that of disciplinary specialist colleagues may often be perceived as lower (Mahendra, 2020) because of the very nature of LSP as "a service industry for other specialisms" (Hutchinson & Waters, 1987, p. 164) at institutions where language studies are not a core discipline. This implies cooperation that is not based on an equal partnership between two colleagues but a relationship between a superordinate disciplinary teacher and a subordinate LSP teacher.

3.7. LSP communities of practice

If a disciplinary community is described as a discourse community of members that share the same objectives (Charles & Pecorari, 2016), then the LSP disciplinary community consists of all those stakeholders that are involved in LSP in any way. These include first and foremost the LSP learners and LSP teachers, but also disciplinary teachers, management of institutions that provide LSP instruction, present of future employers of the LSP learners, national and international governmental policy-makers, and so on.

The professional development of LSP teachers also largely depends on their engagement in and belonging to the LSP community of practice and/or research, which has a significant effect on the development of their professional identity (Meihami & Werbińska, 2022). In other words, this refers to the contact and cooperation with other LSP teachers within the national community or internationally. Therefore, in this subchapter we will have a look at the cohesive elements of the community of LSP teachers: associations, conferences, and journals. Another significant element, which also corroborates the support to the LSP community at the political level, is projects targeting the professional development of LSP teachers. These are presented in a dedicated chapter of this book.

LSP teachers may be members of the community of LSP teachers by joining one or several national and/or international associations of LSP teachers. In Slovenia, this is the Slovene Association of LSP Teachers. Since its establishment in 1997, it "has been dedicated to creating linkages and support for LSP teacher professionals in their continuous professional development, as well as developing LSP courses/materials and introducing novel didactical approaches with a view to improving the quality of LSP teaching and learning."[70] On the other hand, no association that would be specifically dedicated to LSP teachers exists in Poland. Other LSP teacher associations at the national level include, for instance the Croatian Association of LSP Teachers at Higher Education Institutions[71], the French Study and Research Group on English for Specific Purposes[72], and Study and Research Group on Spanish for Specific Purposes[73], the Hungarian Association of Teachers and Researchers of Languages for Specific Purposes[74], the Spanish Association of Applied Linguistics[75], the British Association of Lecturers in English for Academic Purposes[76], and the Asia-Pacific LSP and Professional Communication Association[77], to name just a few.

Several among the needs of LSP teachers can also be catered for by national or international associations, or institutes of applied linguistics. The Institute of Applied Linguistics at the Adam Mickiewicz University, Poznań, in Poland[78], for instance, aims to combine research and teaching in teacher education and professional development, translation studies, and communication and mediation studies, while their projects also focus on disciplinary language teaching, and the functions and structure of functional texts. Both can be found among the core professional development needs of LSP teachers (Jurkovič et al., 2023).

In addition to LSP teacher associations at the national level, there are also several international associations, for example the European Association of Languages for Specific Purposes[79], and the International ESP Teachers' Association[80]. Most of these associations provide a meeting point for LSP teachers whose teaching is embedded in a variety of disciplines. However, there are also associations that are dedicated to LSP teaching in specific disciplines. Two examples are the European Association of Language Teachers for Healthcare[81] and the International Maritime English Conference[82].

---

70 http://eng.sdutsj.si/.
71 http://unjsvu.hr/en/.
72 https://www.geras.fr/.
73 https://www.geres-sup.com/.
74 http://szokoe.hu/?lang=en.
75 http://www.aesla.org.es/es/aesla-english.
76 https://www.baleap.org/.
77 https://www.lsppc.org/.
78 https://amu.edu.pl/en/main-page/amu-directory/faculties/faculty-of-modern-languages-and-literatures/institute-of-applied-linguistics.
79 http://www.aelfe.org.
80 https://esptassociation.com/.
81 https://ealthy.com/.
82 http://www.imla.co/imec/.

One of the main activities of the majority of these associations is the regular organisation of LSP conferences, that provide an important meeting point for LSP teachers and their colleagues from different settings. This is particularly important because many LSP teachers may feel isolated in their institutions and need to create professional links beyond them (Belcher, 2009). A useful resource where these conferences are publicised is the LinguistList website[83] and the websites of each association.

Last but not least, being a member of the LSP teacher community also means regularly following the latest research findings published in academic and professional journals in the fields underlying LSP teaching. In the Social Sciences Citation Index (SSCI) database, these journals are, for instance, Journal of English for Academic Purposes (ISSN: 1475-1585/1878-1497), English for Specific Purposes (ISSN: 0889-4906/1873-1937), and Iberica (ISSN: 1139-7241/2340-2784). In addition to these, research and academic papers investigating LSP topics are published by LSP journals indexed in other databases, as well as journals dedicated to the broader field of research in linguistics and applied linguistics, and general foreign language teaching.

3.8. Synthesis

This chapter is entirely dedicated to LSP teachers, in particular their roles, required competences including disciplinary knowledge, their identity, a presentation of communities of practice, and the challenges that they face to help them develop the former and overcome the latter.

First of all, it was shown that all of the different, complex, changing, and intertwining roles of LSP teachers strongly contest the perception that views all teachers, including LSP teachers, as technicians, and teaching, including LSP teaching, as routine action (Abedeen, 2015). On the contrary, efficient and learner-centred LSP teaching requires a teacher who is able and willing to play a number of different roles dictated by the changing circumstances in LSP classrooms, engendered among other things by rapidly developing ICT and AI technologies and increasing numbers of multicultural classes.

Next, the variety of the competences that LSP teachers need to develop calls for a dedicated, research-based, and validated competence framework for LSP teachers. Undoubtedly, a crucial first step in this direction was made by the partners involved in the Erasmus+ Catapult project with their LSP Teacher

---

83 https://old.linguistlist.org/callconf/browse-current.cfm?type=Conf.

Common Competence Framework[84]. Another relevant resource is BALEAP's (2008) Competency Framework for Teachers of English for Academic Purposes. The next step to make is the upgrading of the flexibility of the proposed framework so that it would accommodate different disciplines, and educational and language proficiency levels, as well as the transversal skills whose importance seems to be increasing exponentially.

LSP teacher identity is a complex concept that is closely related to LSP teacher roles and competences. As a result of these, therefore, we may assume that the identity of LSP teachers may, on the one hand, in part overlap with the identity of LGP teachers and, on the other, also be different from it. In addition, the predominant role of ESP and ESP compared with the roles of other LSPs used for occupational or academic purposes also implies that ESP teachers' identities might overlap with but also differ from the identities of teachers of other LSPs.

The discussion of the challenges faced by LSP teachers reveals two important issues. The first one is that the challenges faced by LSP teachers today are similar to the challenges faced by LSP teachers four decades ago. This seems to corroborate what has been mentioned several times in this book, i.e., the insufficient attention dedicated to LSP teacher education and professional development then and now. The second issue is that the challenges faced by LSP teachers are not localised or, in other words, limited to a single geographical context. On the contrary, the same challenges have to be dealt with by LSP teachers in different geographical and educational contexts, and at national and international levels.

Last but not least, this chapter emphasises the importance of the LSP community of practice as a cohesive element that provides LSP teachers with opportunities for professional development through community engagement in associations, conferences, and journals, to mention only the most salient opportunities. In fact, these may provide a significant national and international support network for LSP teachers, especially those teaching less widely taught LSPs embedded in less widely taught disciplines.

---

84 http://catapult-project.eu/wp-content/uploads/2019/11/CATAPULT_LSP_Teacher_CCF_v12.pdf.

4. LSP teacher professional development projects

4.1. Introduction

This chapter is an overview of the existing projects dedicated to the problem of LSP teacher education and professional development, and is an answer to the incongruence between the profiles of those seeking for a job in LSP teaching on the one hand, and the required skills needed in the LSP teaching sector on the other (Chateaureynaud & John, 2023). In that sense, the presentation of the three projects: TRAILs, Catapult, and LSP-TEOC.Pro should be understood as the presentation of initial attempts to develop solutions to the under-researched, even non-existent area of standardised LSP teacher education and professional development in Europe. The following subchapters will discuss each of the three project's objectives, partnership, intellectual outputs, and results.

4.2. TRAILs

Project website: https://trails.hypotheses.org/

The Erasmus+ LSP Teacher Training Summer School (TRAILs) (2018-1- FR01-KA203-048085) project was based on LSP teacher education and professional development and aimed at the development of skills to encourage and support high quality and innovation in LSP teaching. Both quantitative and qualitative methodologies were adopted to analyse and describe the state of current provision of LSP teacher education and professional development programmes in the EHEA and the authentic professional development needs as seen by in-service LSP teachers. During the TRAILS project, the gap between existing LSP teacher education and professional development provision and the needs of LSP teachers provided the grounds for the definition of the professional development objectives, topic areas, and learning outcomes for an LSP teacher professional development summer school (Chateaureynaud & John, 2023). Initially, the project, which started in 2018, was to end with the TRAILs summer school in September 2020, but due to the Covid-19 pandemic the duration of the project was extended to 2021, and a winter school was organised instead in February, 2021.

The eight partners involved in the TRAILs project were:
- Université de Bordeaux (France) as the Project Coordinator,
- Arcola Research llp (United Kingdom),
- Jade Hochschule Wilhelmshaven (Germany),
- Sveučilište u Zagrebu, Fakultet strojarstva i brodogradnje (Croatia),
- Universidad de Cadiz (Spain),
- Università degli Studi di Bergamo (Italy),
- Uniwersytet im. Adama Mickiewicza W Poznaniu (Poland), and
- Univerza v Ljubljani (Slovenia).

The intellectual outputs of the TRAILS project with their main results are presented in Table 10.

Table 10. Description of TRAILS intellectual outputs (IOs)[85]

IO number	IO title	IO description
1	Identification and analysis of LSP teacher training programmes in Europe	Defining the situation of specialised language teaching in the European Higher Education Area (EHEA).
2	Identification of LSP teacher needs	Analysis of LSP teacher needs with special focus on required qualifications, teaching skills, use of ICT, knowledge of the discipline, etc.
3	Definition of training outcomes based on identified gaps between LSP provision in Europe and LSP teacher needs	Identifying of a gap between the needs and the current situation in LSP teacher training
4	Innovative LSP teacher training curriculum	Designing of LSP teacher training curriculum based on the gap identified in IO3
5	Evaluation report, methodology and toolkit	Describing the project's methodology and the quality of conducted activities.

The main results of the research achieved in the two first IOs delivered important information about the state of LSP teacher education and professional development in the EHEA. Despite a noticeable increase in interest in LSP didactics, in

---

[85] https://trails.hypotheses.org/.

practice LSP teacher education is given a marginal role. Only 8% of all higher education institutions surveyed, and offering modern languages, provide some kind of LSP teacher education and professional development. Moreover, the curricula examined display essential differences in both form and content (John et al., 2023; Kic-Drgas & Woźniak, 2022a, 2022b). On the one hand, higher education institutions do not provide any LSP teacher SP teacher education and professional development programmes, on the other, the existing programmes are far from standardised and differ in initial requirements, literature, form of activities, and so on. All in all, LSP teacher education and professional development in the EHEA needs further research and, above all, standardisation and unification. An observation common for all courses is the popularity of the use of various ICT tools for motivating students and enhancing the attractiveness of the course.

In the course of IO2, quantitative and qualitative data were collected from 621 LSP teachers from 33 EHEA countries. The results helped to identify 62 LSP teacher needs but also revealed LSP teacher education and professional development gaps that match some of the findings highlighted in the preceding IO1 report.[86]

Below are the identified LSP teacher professional development needs that Jurkovič et al. (2023) defined as core (see also Bocanegra-Valle & Perea-Barbera, 2023) (Table 11).

Table 11. Core professional development needs of LSP teachers and consensus rate among survey respondents (Jurkovič et al., 2023; see also Bocanegra-Valle & Perea-Barbera, 2023)

Core professional development need	Total (%)
Analysis of target and learner needs	97
LSP vocabulary teaching	97
Materials design and development	96
Awareness of the context of the discipline	96
Course design and development	94
General principles about LSP	94
Task-based teaching	94
Genres of the discipline	94
Content-based teaching (CBT)	92
Materials evaluation	92
LSP challenges, opportunities and constraints	92
Lesson planning	91
Teaching methodologies	91
Learning strategies	91
Teacher and student motivation	91
Assessment methods	91
Information communication technologies (ICT)	90

---

86 https://trails.hypotheses.org/files/2023/01/IO2_Identification-of-LSP-teacher-needs.pdf.

Table 11 *(Continued)*

Core professional development need	Total (%)
Skills teaching	90
Syllabus design and development	89
Autonomous and self-directed learning	89
Testing practices	89
Knowledge of the discipline and training	88
Self-study, critical thinking and student autonomy	86
Group work and group management	86
Engagement in LSP communities of practice	86
Content and language integrated learning (CLIL)	85
Classroom management and practice	85

Compiling the results of IO1 and IO2, the following 6-pillar model was constructed based on the gaps between LSP teacher education and professional development in the EHEA and LSP teacher needs (Figure 14).

LSP teacher education and professional development					
Needs analysis	Learning objectives	Materials and methods	Evaluation	LSP in general	Transversal skills

Figure 14. 6-pillar model of LSP teacher education and professional development

This model became the framework for designing the final event of the TRAILS project, i.e., the winter school for LSP teachers. The first implementation took place from 22–26 February 2021. Because of the Covid-19 pandemic it was held online. The event involved a total of 31 international participants, including 13 LSP teachers and 18 students from seven countries (Croatia, France, Italy, Poland, Slovenia, Spain, and the United Kingdom).[87] The curriculum of the Winter School included activities based on the needs of LSP teachers that emerged during the interviews and questionnaires that formed the initial phase of the project. Each day of the school started with a theoretical, interactive introduction, followed by a practical part during which the participants could test the presented content in a practical way (see Figure 15).[88]

---

87 https://trails.hypotheses.org/training-events.
88 https://trails.hypotheses.org/training-events.

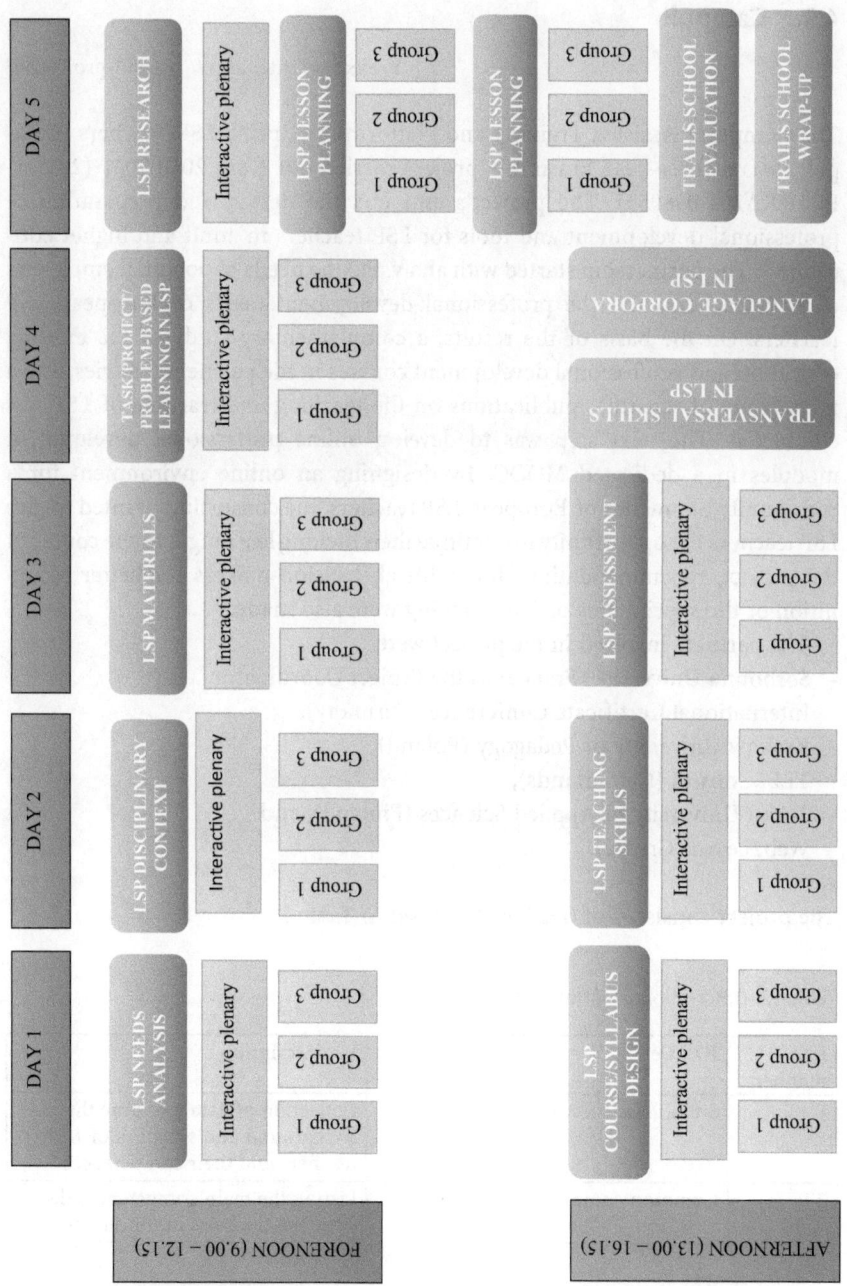

Figure 15. TRAILS curriculum (TRAILS, 2021)

4.3. Catapult

Project website: http://catapult-project.eu/

The Computer Assisted Training and Platforms to Upskill LSP Teachers (Catapult) was a three-year Erasmus+ project carried out from 2018-2021 (2018-1-FR01-KA204-048053). The project's aim was the design and preparation of professional development and tools for LSP teachers in adult and higher education[89]. The partnership started with analysing the needs of potential employers of LSP teachers, and the professional development needs of European LSP teachers. On the basis of the results, a complementary study of the existing education and professional development courses in the partner countries, and a meta-study of scientific publications on the teaching and learning of LSP was conducted. The next step was to develop online professional development modules in a dedicated MOOC. By designing an online environment for a community of practice of European LSP teachers, the consortium wanted to give LSP teachers the opportunity to continue their lifelong learning.[90] In the course of the project, recommendations for political decision-makers for better recognition of the specificities of LSP teaching were also made.

The partners involved in the project were:
- Sorbonne Université (France) as the Project Coordinator,
- International Certificate Conference (Germany),
- Krakow University of Pedagogy (Poland),
- TELLConsult (Netherlands),
- Turku University of Applied Sciences (Finland), and
- Web2Learn (Greece).

The project consisted of five IOs described in Table 12.[91]

Table 12. Description of Catapult IOs[92]

IO number	IO title	IO description
1	Situational survey	Collection of data to define the background and situation of LSP teachers and their competences
2	Common competence framework	Listing the main competences defined on the basis of the survey

---

89 http://catapult-project.eu/category/news/.
90 https://erasmus-plus.ec.europa.eu/projects/search/details/2018-1-FR01-KA204-048053.
91 http://catapult-project.eu.
92 http://catapult-project.eu.

Table 12 *(Continued)*

IO number	IO title	IO description
3	MOOC	Designing of a Massive Online Open Course (MOOC) to develop and train competences defined in IO1
4	Community of practice platform	Creating a platform to share and discuss the results of the project and possible implementation in work-related environment
5	Accreditation	Monitoring the quality of the project and accreditation of the achieved results

The main results coming from the research in IO1 highlight the importance of ICT skills in the educational sector but the comparison of needs and demands showed a gap between the development of ICT skills at the university level (only 12% of the language teachers benefited from ICT courses and events during their studies and almost half of the interviewees picked up the necessary ICT skills on-the-job). The interviewed LSP teachers in particular pointed out the difficulty of accessing teaching materials that, on the one hand, included specific language features and, on the other hand, contained elements of the respective discipline. At the same time, disciplinary knowledge appeared to be extremely important for recruiters in the labour market. In order to deal with this mismatch, collaboration between LSP teachers, and the ability to use Internet resources in the form of OER was essential. Another problem pointed out by LSP teachers was their marginalisation, and the lack of communities or discussion platforms that would allow for effective collaboration and exchange of ideas.

As a result of surveys, market analysis and interviews, as well as a rigorous literature review, the participants in the project developed the LSP Teacher Common Competence Framework[93], a document describing the core competences of LSP teachers, consisting of five competence areas: "general teaching competences, collaboration and intercultural mediation competences, analytical competences, course/material-design competences and evaluation competences"[94].

The result of IO3 was an 8-week course delivered by a group of experts in LSP and Computer-Assisted Language Learning comprising 7 modules, which could be enrolled on at three levels: Browser Level, allowing reading the course mate-

---

93 http://catapult-project.eu/wp-content/uploads/2019/11/CATAPULT_LSP_Teacher_CCF_v12.pdf.
94 http://catapult-project.eu/wp-content/uploads/2019/11/CATAPULT_LSP_Teacher_CCF_v12.pdf.

rials and gaining an insight into LSP pedagogy without doing the quizzes or more complex assignments, Tester Level, at which scoring 50% on all quizzes is needed to be awarded the badges, and finally the Creator Level, which ends with a certificate after completing all assignments and quizzes.[95]

As a way to combat the marginalisation of LSP teachers and enhance community spirit, two tools were developed as a result of IO4: "a Community of Practice platform named LinguaCoP, with the following features: Forum, Blog, Notifications and Resource Inventory, in which freelance adult education language teachers as well as higher education language teachers, especially in the field of LSP education, can meet, discuss best practices, find academic publications."[96] and "a matching tool named Linguaclick that aims to connect individual language learners with companies seeking language teachers to employ, and Higher Education institutions looking for language teachers."[97] The partners of the project also formulated a list of potential challenges for LSP teachers, such as student/teacher demotivation, encouraging the company or institution to recognise necessary change in the LSP sector, and the application of all the new tools that might partly be replacing face to face classes.

4.4. LSP-TEOC.PRO

Project website: https://lsp-teoc-pro.de/

A three-year Erasmus+ project titled LSP Teacher Education Online Course for Professional Development (LSP-TEOC.Pro) ran from 2020 to 2023 (2020-1-DE01-KA203-005687). The LSP TEOC.PRO project relied on the LSP teacher education curriculum developed in the TRAILs project, on the basis of which the LSP-TEOC.Pro OER was developed for future LSP teachers as a response to the need for standardised solutions for the pre-service education of future LSP teachers and professional development of in-service LSP teachers. A very important part of the project is the fact that the OER is available in seven languages, including Polish and Slovene, which means that it is a tool for all LSP teachers, regardless of the LSP taught, and not just for teachers using English, for which the teaching materials and resources are mainly developed.

The nine partners involved in the LSP-TEOC.Pro project were:
– Jade Hochschule Wilhelmshaven/Oldenburg/Elsfleth (Germany), as the project Coordinator,
– Arcola Research llp (United Kingdom),

---

[95] http://catapult-project.eu/output-3/.
[96] http://catapult-project.eu/wp-content/uploads/2022/01/AXX_O4A5_report.pdf, 11.06.2023.
[97] http://catapult-project.eu/wp-content/uploads/2022/01/AXX_O4A5_report.pdf.

- Çukurova Üniversitesi (Turkey),
- Sveučilište u Zagrebu, Fakultet strojarstva i brodogradnje (Croatia),
- Université de Bordeaux (France),
- Universidad de Cadiz (Spain),
- Università degli Studi di Bergamo (Italy),
- Uniwersytet im. Adama Mickiewicza W Poznaniu (Poland), and
- Univerza v Ljubljani (Slovenia).

The project consisted of eight IOS presented in Table 13.

Table 13. Description of LSP-TEOC.PRO intellectual outputs (IOs)[98,99]

IO number	IO title	IO description
1	Analysis and synthesis of existing LSP teacher training and development programmes	To analyse and synthesise existing LSP teacher training and development programmes based on existing on-campus and online materials for LSP teacher training and professional development in the European higher education areas.
2	Definition of an online teaching methodology	To review online learning methodologies, activities and technologies to look for significant examples for practice.
3	Development of course content for LSP teacher training and development	To develop course content based on templates which have been implemented for the purpose of efficient integration into the online course. The templates guarantee a consistent format and very little variation amongst the different implementation languages (i.e., Croatian, English, French, German, Italian, Polish, Slovenian, Spanish and Turkish).
4	Implementation of online course for new LSP teacher training development on Internet platform	To integrate into the selected learning management systems (LMS) self-registration, quizzes and individual feedback, and solve usability issues.
5	Piloting developed LSP teacher training online course	To pilot the entire course among participants from the project consortium member countries.

---

98 https://lsp-teoc-pro.de/.
99 LSP-TEOC.Pro application form.

Table 13 *(Continued)*

IO number	IO title	IO description
6	Trailing developed LSP teacher training online course	Formulation of learning analytics methods on the data gathered during the large-scale trialling phase of the project.
7	Analysis of trialling user data and application of learning analytics	The data include the users' nationality, affiliation, status (e.g., student, early career, experienced practitioner), their choice of their learning content, the dedication time to the different course contents, the correctness of the quizzes, to name but a few. In this intellectual output, typical groups of users identified with the aim to develop individualised pathways through the online course.
8	Methodologies/guidelines – Evaluation method and tool	Evaluation design and plan for the project, including the 'internal' evaluation, process evaluation and summative (outcomes) evaluation.

First, existing online courses in the field of LSP teacher education and professional development were identified and analysed. The data collection questionnaire used for this purpose consisted of items for the analysis of websites of universities and research institutions in order to find online courses on the education and professional development of LSP teachers. The project partners analysed 532 websites of universities, faculties, and other accredited institutions. In the five European countries analysed (Croatia, Germany, Italy, Poland, and Spain) and 532 websites visited, only 12 online LSP teacher education and development programmes were found. The data reveal that eight of the online programmes are commercial in nature, while no information is available for three programmes. In addition, it was found that ten of the online programmes were designed for beginner LSP teachers, nine were designed for experienced LSP teachers with more than five years' experience, eleven were designed for LGP teachers, and three were designed for general language students. However, although most of these online programmes are suitable for LSP teachers, they do not qualify participants to teach LSP or only partially qualify them. The qualifications obtained after completing the online programmes are also quite diverse. From the data obtained, it can be clearly concluded that online courses, as forms of LSP teacher education and professional development, are very rare and do not fill the research and teaching gap.

In order to meet the ever-growing needs of LSP teacher education and professional development, as well as to increase the availability of free content related to this topic, the project partners undertook preparatory work for the development of an OER platform which would be accessible to LSP teachers teaching a variety of specialist languages and could also offer content in different languages.

The course is designed to cover 48 hours of student workload and consists of the following seven modules, which can be taken in any order (Figure 16):

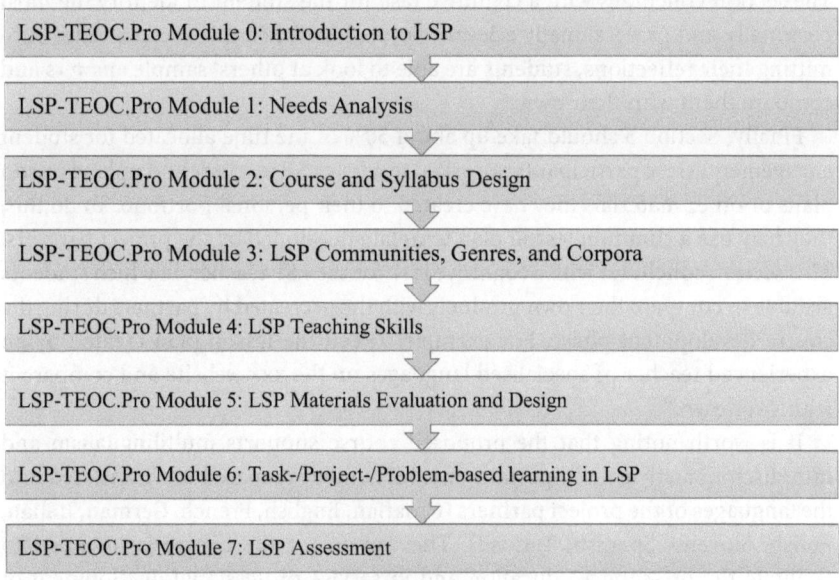

Figure 16. Content of online course LSP-TEOC.Pro[100]

Each module is divided into three main sections: the theoretical section, the LSP learner section, and the LSP teacher section.

The theoretical section covers approximately 25% of the time allocated for student engagement. The main purpose of this section is to provide students with the theoretical knowledge they need to work on the tasks in Sections 2 and 3. The theoretical material is divided into short sections presented in the form of a multimedia presentation. Each theoretical presentation is followed by a set of comprehension questions on the main topics that are important to remember. The first part also includes a video recorded by an experienced LSP teacher with practical tips or good practices on how to incorporate the topic described into the LSP classroom.

---

100 https://lsp-teoc-pro.de/.

Next, Section 2 in which the student undertakes the role of LSP learner should take up approximately 25% of the student's engagement time with the module. It is divided into Parts A and B. Part A is intended for novice LSP teachers. In this part, the most important concepts from the theoretical part of the module will be repeated and extended. In Part B, the student takes on the role of LSP teacher and is asked to complete specific tasks to be able to reflect on the new knowledge acquired and on the process of LSP learning. The tasks in this section address the development of skills and language elements at receptive and productive levels. The section concludes with a cognitive task for the student to identify the most personally and professionally relevant points learned in this section. After submitting their reflections, students are able to look at others' sample answers and compare them with their own.

Finally, Section 3 should take up about 50% of the time allocated for student engagement. Here participants are asked to act as LSP teachers and upload lesson plans or other materials they have created to their personal portfolio. To do this, they may use a common lesson plan template developed by the project partners. This section concludes with a cognitive task for the LSP teacher, in which students are able to compare their own products with those created by partners during the course development phase. For example: "Read the lesson plan created by an experienced teacher of specialised languages on the xxx website and compare it with your own."

It is worth noting that the proposed course supports multilingualism and interdisciplinarity in an important way. All content prepared was translated into the languages of the project partners (Croatian, English, French, German, Italian, Polish, Slovene, Spanish, Turkish). The content of the course is intended to facilitate the pre-service education and in-service professional development of LSP teachers for various LSPs. In addition, the course content does not focus on one specific area of knowledge but touches on various disciplines, for instance technology, medicine, business, water management, and so on. By planning the content and form of the course in this way, the project partners aimed to demonstrate the importance of developing the individual competences associated with the profession of an LSP teacher.

> "More than 300 participants in total tested the course at various stages of its development, including 183 participants in its final form. The course students from Croatia, France, Germany, Italy, Poland, Slovenia, Spain, Turkey ranged from those with long and extensive experience as LSP teachers to newcomers who are just preparing for the profession."[101]

---

101 https://lsp-teoc-pro.de/booklet/.

Following learning analytics, the participants can be divided into the following groups[102]:
- pragmatists-perfectionists (spend time carefully completing all available tasks),
- pragmatists-fast learners (limit the time spent on completing the tasks to the minimum),
- deep learners-perfectionists (also complete additional tasks), and
- deep learners-fast learners (complete only compulsory tasks to obtain the certificate).

The most popular modules were Modules 0, 1 and 2. The participants defined the course as beneficial, insightful, enlightening, and thought provoking. The results showed that there was a statistically significant difference between the scores achieved in the pre-tests and post-tests of all modules, which demonstrates the efficiency of the course.

A system of badges was introduced into the OER, which are a kind of award for the student's achievement in the form of correct completion of a task. Tasks marked with a badge are compulsory for the student to receive the certificate.

4.5. Synthesis

This chapter is devoted to an overview of recent projects on the subject of LSP teaching. The chapter presents three projects: TRAILS, Catapult, and LSP-TEOC.Pro. All three projects respond to the ever-growing needs for experienced and future LSP teachers in Europe, and indicate the growing political support to LSP teacher education and professional development at the EU level. The research carried out within the domain of these projects and the resources delivered should be seen as contributions to further research and action in response to the growing needs of LSP education and professional development.

The TRAILS project was set up to investigate the needs of LSP teachers and to contrast them with authentic LSP teacher education programmes in Europe in order to identify existing gaps. The most important findings of the survey were to highlight the lack of standardisation in the education and professional development of LSP teachers in Europe; the programmes analysed in the survey at more than one thousand institutions vary in terms of the number of ECTS credits awarded, length, form of credit, length, recommended working methods, and the use of ICT. It can be concluded that although a visible increase in interest in LSP teaching can be recorded, also in recent academic publications, in practical terms LSP teacher education and professional development is still treated marginally

---

102 https://lsp-teoc-pro.de/booklet/.

(Kic-Drgas & Wozniak, 2022a). On the other hand, interviews with in-service teachers indicated deficits in further professional development opportunities, needs in terms of course design, lesson planning, knowledge and use of text genres specific to the discipline, use of action-oriented teaching methods in language teaching, proper assessment of material, and soft competences. The outcome of the course was the delivery of online LSP teacher education and professional development (originally intended to be classroom-based, unfortunately due to the Covid-19 pandemic it was replaced by a remote format) based on diagnosed needs.

The Catapult project was also based on a qualitative and quantitative analysis of the needs of LSP teachers in terms of the competences necessary for effective LSP teaching. ICT skills in the educational sector proved to be of significant importance, however the comparison of needs and demands showed a gap between the development of ICT skills at the higher education level. In addition, aspects such as lack of specialised knowledge, institutional support, in-service education provision and necessary tools and materials were found. The data collected in the project were used to prepare a MOOC aimed at developing those proficiencies identified as lacking by the LSP teachers surveyed.

The third project – LSP.TEOC-Pro – is a continuation of the TRAILs project, and primarily aimed at analysing online education and professional development opportunities for LSP teachers. As a result of the survey, an online course was developed which, due to its complex and multi-layered structure, provides in-service professional development for experienced language teachers as well as pre-service education for future teachers. The project investigated online teacher education provision and, based on the needs of in-service and future LSP teachers, developed a multilingual course offering seven sections on basic areas of LSP teaching. The innovative character of the course is demonstrated by the possibility of obtaining a certificate and the choice of a personalised path for more and less advanced LSP teachers.

5. LSP teacher education and professional development

5.1. Introduction

Despite the increasing availability of LSP courses and the resulting demand for qualified LSP teachers (Ding & Campion, 2016; Grosse & Voght, 2012; Szymańska-Tworek & Makowska-Songin, 2019), there is a shortage of pre-service education and in-service professional development programmes for LSP teachers throughout the EHEA, as has been highlighted at many points in this book. In addition, the programmes that are available mostly rely on the experience and assumptions of their creators rather than on robust empirical data (Bocanegra-Valle & Basturkmen, 2019). Also as a result of the communicative approach to language teaching, which put learner needs to the forefront, the professional development needs of LSP teachers used to be neglected (Bocanegra-Valle, 2016; Flowerdew, 2013).

It has been shown that LSP teachers may have different pre-service education and in-service professional development needs than LGP teachers (Bocanegra-Valle and Basturkmen, 2019; Bocanegra-Valle & Perea-Barbera, 2023; Jurkovič et al., 2023; López-Zurita & Vázquez-Amador, 2023; Podgoršek et al., 2021). However, all the studies made into the professional development needs of LSP teachers to date relied on quantitative and qualitative data provided by LSP teachers about their own community. This means that, to date, research has neglected another important stakeholder in the process of foreign language teacher education, in particular in the pre-service education before foreign language teachers start their teaching careers: these are the pre-service teacher educators or, in other words, those experts in language teaching methodology that prepare students for their future careers as foreign language teachers, both within LSP or LGP domains.

Therefore, to bridge this research gap and provide a holistic view of the professional development needs of LSP teachers, the objective of our qualitative research presented in this chapter was to explore the views of foreign language teacher educators on the pre-service education and in-service professional development of LSP teachers. Particular focus was placed on the pre-service foreign language teacher educators' views on the similarities and differences between the pre-service education of future LSP and LGP teachers and their later continuous professional development, the development of disciplinary knowledge, and the role of collaboration at all stages of the pre-service education and in-service professional development of LSP teachers.

5.2. Literature review

Demand for LSP courses has been increasing (Ding & Campion, 2016; Grosse & Voght, 2012; Szymańska-Tworek & Makowska-Songin, 2019), which has led to the resulting increased need for qualified LSP teachers (Hüttner et al., 2009; Marra, 2013). However, most LSP teachers still begin their LSP teaching careers, assuming a wide variety of LSP specific roles, without any previous pre-service education or in-service support (Paltridge, 2013).

Teacher education can broadly be divided into initial or pre-service education, and on-going or continuous professional development (Basturkmen, 2014). The latter will take place throughout the teaching career. Generally speaking, an LSP teacher's expertise and competences will significantly develop through learning-by-doing, on-the-job, which implies that pre-service education courses need to provide the groundwork for the motivation and life-long learning ability of teachers (Skela, 2019). Charles and Pecorari (2016) agree that although the scope and depth of the knowledge that an LSP teacher needs to possess might be daunting, it can be acquired on the way if the LSP teacher makes a commitment to lifelong professional development.

The relative absence or systemic incoherence of pre-service or in-service LSP teacher education programmes was clearly shown by John et al. (2023) through the findings of a research study that scanned more than 1,000 institutions in 25 EHEA countries. The aim of the study was to collect and analyse basic information and learning outcomes of any available accredited LSP teacher education programme in the EHEA. The findings indicated that LSP teacher education in some form is provided in 14 analysed countries. However, these programmes vary significantly in terms of scope, content, and format. The latter ranges from complete courses to modules (the prevalent format), subjects, and other educational formats. LSP teacher education courses or modules are mostly elective, which means that students do not need to choose them as mandatory courses if they do not wish to. Most programmes provide education for future teachers of English as an LSP, followed by German, Spanish, and some French, and Russian. The entry requirements also vary, so do the language competence levels that the candidates are supposed to have at enrolment. The descriptions of the programmes reveal that different teaching methodologies are adopted for LSP teacher education but no predominant methodology can be identified. Therefore, it can be concluded that LSP teacher education in the EHEA is not absent. However, it is characterised by a total lack of consistency, systematicity, or standardisation.

As will be reiterated in the following sections, the LSP teacher education programmes that do exist, however, are based on the experience and assumptions of their creators rather than on robust empirical data (Bocanegra-Valle & Basturkmen, 2019). Three models that can provide some methodological starting points for the design of systematically organised LSP teacher education programmes are presented below.

Hüttner et al. (2009) based their LSP teacher education model at the University of Vienna on the assumption that it is impossible to predict which LSPs preservice LSP teachers will be expected to teach in their future professional lives. Therefore, LSP teacher education should empower them with the competences (rather than skills) to autonomously analyse any LSP genre, which will help them deal with any specific, unpredicted teaching situations. The aim of this educational model therefore is to provide a genre-informed and genre-centred teaching approach that will enable future LSP teachers to familiarise with any genre and to use this knowledge in teaching. The main premise that this model is based on is that genre analysis and corpus linguistics should feature centrally in an LSP teacher education model. As a result, a genre- and corpus-based approach was developed as a form of bridge between applied linguistics theory and teaching methodology, with the overall aim to incorporate genre analysis and corpus linguistics findings into the education of pre-service LSP teachers.

Krajka (2018) investigated the relevance of a research-based approach to LSP teacher education, in which pre-service LSP teachers acted as researchers in conducting needs analysis, materials evaluation, and digital materials development for contexts in professional domains that they themselves selected. The whole process consisted of six stages: the conceptualisation of the discipline was followed by the design of needs analysis instruments, the collection and understanding of needs analysis data, the selection of the digital environment and tools that were used for materials development, the creation of digital teaching and learning materials, and peer-to-peer presentation and evaluation of course materials developed as a result of this process. The findings indicated that the needs analysis process was the least problematic element. However, the pre-service LSP teachers experienced most difficulties as a result of the lack of disciplinary knowledge when they needed to define the learning outcomes, find authentic materials, and develop course materials based on these. Krajka (2018) advocates for more systematic LSP teacher education courses that would include actual fieldwork tasks, through which pre-service LSP teachers could develop autonomy in needs analysis, course and syllabus design, and materials development. Given that digital and self-directed learning have become essential for any kind of learning, e-learning courses have become a practical option for LSP teacher education.

Last but not least, Kirkgöz (2019) relied on constructivism as the main paradigm in LSP teacher education to propose and evaluate a model for pre-service LSP teacher education in Turkey. The course consisted of two main components. The first one consisted of lectures accompanied by group or pair work tasks on needs analysis, materials design, course design, and so on, which enabled the students to acquire the necessary theoretical foundations. The second component was fieldwork in which each group of students designed an LSP course in a selected domain, developed a lesson plan, and provided examples of teaching. This allowed the students to apply theoretical knowledge on the meaning and importance of LSP, needs analysis, and materials design in practical situations. The findings indicated that the pre-service LSP teachers developed significant knowledge and skills for LSP teaching, and agreed that they felt confident in their abilities to adapt to different teaching contexts and domains.

To enable the integration of the results of the present chapter with previous recent studies into the professional development needs of LSP teachers (Bocanegra-Valle and Basturkmen, 2019; Bocanegra-Valle & Perea-Barbera, 2023; Jurkovič et al., 2023; López-Zurita & Vázquez-Amador, 2023; Podgoršek et al., 2021) and thus provide a holistic view of the professional development needs of LSP teachers, the main findings of these studies will now be summarised.

Bocanegra-Valle and Basturkmen (2019) provided the first empirical (qualitative) study that thoroughly examined LSP teacher professional development needs and laid the groundwork for further research and classification. The aim of their study was to identify and classify the professional development needs of 19 experienced in-service ESP teachers at two Spanish universities, and to contribute to the understanding of the attitudes that higher education ESP teachers have toward ESP teaching, the required knowledge and skills of an ESP higher education teacher, and the peer and systemic support that they would perceive as useful. Five main categories of ESP teacher professional development needs, which can be generalised to the whole LSP context, were derived from the interviewees' responses (Figure 17).

The first category, course development needs, is the largest. It is further subdivided into needs assessment (needs-based instruction is seen as of the cornerstones of ESP teaching), teaching skills (LSP teaching should be based on authentic activities and matched with the teaching content), autonomy, materials use and development (based on authentic language use in the related discipline), and motivation.

Literature review

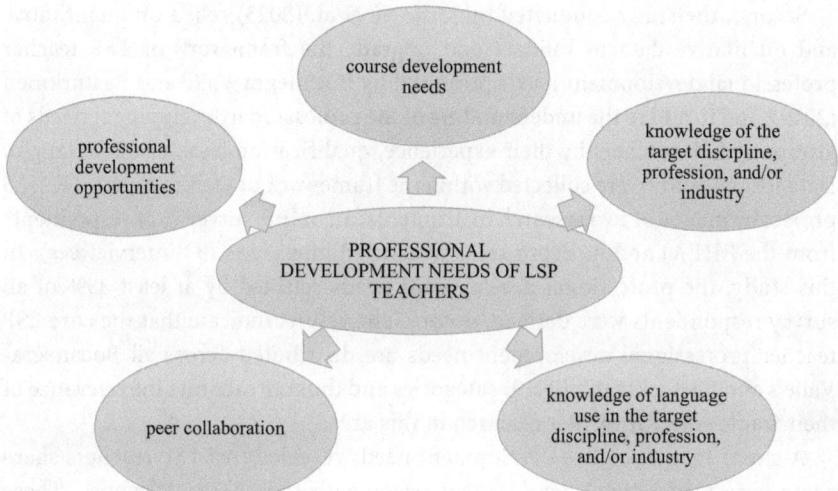

Figure 17. Professional development needs of LSP teachers (Bocanegra-Valle & Basturkmen, 2019)

The second category consists of the knowledge of the target discipline, profession, and/or industry, and participation in the disciplinary community. The latter proved to be essential or highly necessary for most interviewees also because it increases the LSP teacher's confidence and credibility in the broader professional community.

The third category, knowledge of language use in the target discipline, profession, and/or industry, is further subdivided into situational language, situational vocabulary, genres and text types, and disciplinary culture awareness. Therefore, in addition to language knowledge, pedagogical knowledge, and disciplinary knowledge, what is needed is the knowledge of how language is practically used in specific contexts, and discourse and genre analysis skills.

The fourth category, peer collaboration, consists of collaboration with LSP peers and discipline teachers. In fact, most interviewees expressed the need for greater collaboration with other LSP teachers (for instance, through peer tutoring or peer observation) as well as disciplinary teachers (for instance through discussing disciplinary knowledge, problems, or practices).

The fifth category, professional development opportunities, is further subdivided into support for novice and experienced teachers, and their continuous professional development. All interviewees voiced the need for some sort of support during their careers, and almost all mentioned the need for continuous professional development. An important finding is that with career development the needs of LSP teachers will change and so will the ways in which these needs can be met.

Second, the study conducted by Jurkovič et al. (2023) relied on quantitative and qualitative data to validate and upgrade the framework of LSP teacher professional development needs proposed by Bocanegra-Valle and Basturkmen (2019), and to add to the understanding of the professional development needs of groups of LSP teachers by their experience, qualification level, and LSP taught. Data for the study were collected within the framework of the Erasmus+ TRAILS project by means of two research instruments: an online survey (624 respondents from the EHEA) and in-depth semi-structured interviews (33 interviewees). In this study, the professional development needs selected by at least 85% of all survey respondents were defined as core. The results indicate that the core LSP teacher professional development needs are distributed across all Bocanegra-Valle's and Basturkmen's (2019) categories and thus corroborate the relevance of their framework for further research in this area.

A closer look at course development needs revealed that LSP teachers share some core professional development needs with their LGP colleagues. These include, for instance, general teaching methodologies, learning strategies, lesson planning, vocabulary teaching, the use of ICT, skills teaching, self-study, autonomous and self-directed learning, teacher and student motivation, student autonomy, critical thinking, group work management, classroom management, and assessment. However, the same category, i.e., course development needs, includes core knowledge, skills, and competences that are more a requirement for LSP teachers than their LGP colleagues. These are needs analysis, course and syllabus design and development, task-based teaching, content-based teaching, CLIL, materials evaluation and design, and the design of tailor-made achievement tests and the resulting assessment (Jurkovič et al., 2023).

The knowledge of the target discipline/profession/industry is the second category of LSP teacher professional development needs by Bocanegra-Valle and Basturkmen (2019). Interview data reported on in Jurkovič et al. (2023) revealed that knowledge of the target discipline/profession/industry increases the LSP teacher's confidence, implying that disciplinary knowledge or disciplinary acculturation (Chen, 2000) is required for confident and thus effective LSP teaching. The importance of acculturation with the discipline is supported by the need of LSP teachers to have knowledge, skills, and competences in language use in the target discipline/profession/industry. These concern in particular disciplinary genres, their analysis, and final application at the materials design and development stage. Although the relevance of genres in the LSP community has been undisputed, the findings also indicated an unsatisfactory level of awareness of the importance of genres for LSP teaching and learning, at the level of language reception as well as production.

The only core professional development need that referred to peer collaboration as the fourth category of LSP teacher professional development needs is engagement in LSP communities of practice. This possibly represents the need for novice teachers to be mentored by their more experienced colleagues. At later stages of their careers, when their professional development needs change as a result of experience, this might translate into a need for the exchange of good practices and experience with equally experienced peers. The need for collaboration with disciplinary experts produced controversial results. Although this is a core professional development need for some LSP teachers, it does not seem to apply to the majority of the respondents.

Moreover, the results of the study conducted by Jurkovič et al. (2023) only partly corroborate the need for continuous professional development as the fifth category of LSP teachers' professional development needs identified by Bocanegra-Valle and Basturkmen (2019). In fact, only LSP challenges, opportunities and constraints can be found among the needs defined as core.

In addition, Jurkovič et al. (2023) explored the potential differences in the professional development needs of LSP teachers depending on their experience, qualification level, and LSP taught. Experienced and less experienced LSP teachers in the EHEA seem to agree on the vast majority of core LSP teacher professional development needs. The only exception is autonomous and self-directed learning, more highly valued by experienced LSP teachers. Next, if the stances among the holders of doctoral degrees are compared against the same stances among the holders of master's degrees, two statistically significant differences emerge. More holders of doctoral degrees think that an LSP teacher needs knowledge, skills, and competences in ICT. In addition, more doctoral degree holders see research opportunities as one of their core professional development needs. Finally, some differences were observed also depending on the LSP that is taught. ESP teachers seem to attribute a higher value to course design and development, task-based teaching, materials evaluation, and academic discourse. A further relevant finding is that the status and position of LSP teachers of languages other than English is significantly different from that of ESP teachers, for instance in terms of the availability of language corpora, group sizes, language levels, and availability of relevant professional development opportunities, for example conferences or workshops, which proliferate in the world of ESP.

Based on their findings, Jurkovič et al. (2023) propose a three-stage model for LSP teacher development. The first stage should be provided by a general LGP teaching methodology course for pre-service teachers that would cater for those professional development needs that future LSP teachers share with future LGP teachers. The second pre-service stage should consist of a general LSP teaching methodology course that would cater for those core professional development needs that are highly specific to future LSP teachers, and therefore not shared with their LGP colleagues. These core professional development needs include the analysis of target and learner needs, course and syllabus design and development, task- and content-based teaching and CLIL, materials evaluation, materials use and development, specific aspects of assessment and testing, and forms of peer collaboration. The final stage should take the form of discipline-specific acculturation through in-service education under the supervision of an experienced LSP colleague and/or discipline specialist. This stage should mainly cater for those LSP teacher core development needs that cannot be met by courses designed for broader groups of participants coming from different disciplines, namely needs that belong to the 'Knowledge of the target discipline/profession/industry' and 'Knowledge of language use in the target discipline/profession/industry' categories of core LSP teacher professional development needs.

Third, the study conducted by Bocanegra-Valle and Perea-Barberá (2023) relied on the same set of quantitative data collected within the Erasmus+ TRAILS project as Jurkovič et al. (2023). The main findings of their study that complement those reached by Jurkovič et al. (2023) and are relevant for the present chapter are that:
- most respondents did not engage in any formal LSP professional development before or during their teaching careers,
- pre-service LSP teacher education programmes in the EHEA that do exist are far from being standardised,
- most respondents agreed that LSP teacher education and professional development should be required for somebody to receive an LSP teacher qualification,
- most respondents agreed that the professional development needs of LSP teachers are somewhat different from those of LGP teachers although similarities exist,
- the ten most relevant professional development needs as seen by the respondents include the analysis of target and learner needs, LSP vocabulary teaching, materials design and development, disciplinary context awareness, course design and development, lesson planning, general principles of LSP, disciplinary genres, task-based teaching, and materials evaluation, and
- interculturality/internationalisation and English as a *lingua franca* emerged as two additional recurrent professional development needs of LSP teachers.

On the other hand, the study conducted by López-Zurita and Vázquez-Amador (2023) relied on the same set of qualitative data collected within the Erasmus+ TRAILS project as Jurkovič et al. (2023). The main findings of their study that complement those of Jurkovič et al. (2023) and are relevant for the present chapter are that, in the interviewees' opinions:

- LSP teaching is more demanding than LGP teaching because of elements such as discipline-specific vocabulary, materials design, and LSP learner needs analysis,
- LSP teachers learn through their own LSP teaching experience, i.e., on-the-job,
- disciplinary content is a challenge for LSP teachers,
- LSP learners' motivation generally is high, and
- an LSP teacher professional development programme is needed that would promote high-quality and innovative LSP teaching.

The final, fifth, study that will be reported on in this section was conducted by Podgoršek et al. (2021). It aimed to provide an insight into the pre-service education and continuous professional development for LSP teachers in the Slovene higher education area. Syllabus analysis and semi-structured interviews were used as the two main research instruments. First of all, the analysis of the study programmes of language majors at Slovene universities showed that there are no accredited educational programmes for LSP teachers in Slovenia. Next, the interviewed LSP teachers perceive workshops, participation in conferences, autonomous study of literature, and exchange of experiences and opinions as valid opportunities for informal professional improvement. Only one of the interviewees had experience with being mentored by a more experienced colleague. For professional development opportunities to be relevant to them, they must necessarily be based on specific current disciplinary genres, topics, and materials although also events on terminology collection and analysis tools, and the use of ICT were highly valued. Last but not least, the initial stages of their careers as LSP teachers would have been easier if, prior to it, they had received specific education in LSP teaching. Instead, they mostly developed the competences required by LSP teachers while on-the-job, in an autonomous and self-directed way.

5.3. Methodology

5.3.1. Research questions

As mentioned, to date no study has explored the pre-service education and in-service professional development of LSP teachers from the viewpoint of foreign language teacher educators. The research questions posed for this study are as follows:

RQ1: How should the pre-service education of future LSP teachers be similar and/or different from that of the pre-service education of future LGP teachers?

RQ2: Which elements of disciplinary knowledge are important for LSP teachers to have?

RQ3: How and when should the required disciplinary knowledge be developed?

RQ4: How is the continuous professional development of experienced LSP teachers different from that of experienced LGP teachers and how is it similar?

RQ5: What is the role of collaboration in the pre-service education and in-service professional development of LSP teachers?

5.3.2. Instruments and data collection

Data for this study were collected by means of semi-structured interviews, which allow the interviewer to explore unanticipated topics, follow up on interviewees' responses, and collect detailed and context-specific information about the participants' beliefs, attitudes, and behaviours. In this way, the interviewees have the opportunity to express their experiences, realities, and ideas in their own words (Mason, 2002).

The interview protocol was created on the basis of the findings of the previous recent qualitative, quantitative, and mixed-methodology studies outlined above (Bocanegra-Valle and Basturkmen, 2019; Podgoršek et al., 2021; Jurkovič et al., 2023; Bocanegra-Valle and Perea-Barbera, 2023; López-Zurita & Vázquez-Amador, 2023). The aim was to complete the research into LSP teacher professional development needs by exploring the views of foreign language teacher educators, i.e., the educators of future foreign language teachers, on the required pre-service education and in-service professional development of LSP teachers. Therefore, the results of this study will enable the creation of a holistic picture of the professional development needs of LSP teachers from different viewpoints. The interview protocol is presented in Figure 18.

In total, seven foreign language educators from Poland and five from Slovenia were interviewed. If the participant and researcher came from the same geographical area, the interviews were conducted in person. On the other hand, online platforms were used to interview participants from other Polish or Slovene regions. The language used was Polish in the interviews with Polish participants, and Slovene in the interviews with the Slovene participants.

> Dear colleague,
>
> Research has shown that teachers of languages for specific purposes (LSP teachers) may have different pre-service education and in-service professional development needs than the teachers of foreign languages for general purposes (LGP teachers).
>
> The objective of our research is to explore the views of foreign language teacher educators on the required pre-service education and in-service professional development of LSP teachers.
>
> Therefore, we are writing to kindly ask you to take not more than one hour of time for an online meeting for a discussion of questions Q1-Q6 below.
>
> Q1: In your opinion, how should the initial pre-service education of future LSP teachers be different from that of the initial pre-service education of future LGP teachers?
>
> Q2: In your opinion, which elements of disciplinary knowledge (e.g., the knowledge of nursing, business, or engineering) are important for LSP teachers to have?
>
> Q3: In your opinion, how and when should the required disciplinary knowledge be developed?
>
> Q4: In your opinion, how is the continuous professional development of experienced LSP teachers different from that of experienced LGP teachers and how is it similar?
>
> Q5: What is, in your opinion, the role of collaboration in the pre-service education and in-service professional development of LSP teachers?
>
> Q6: After the discussion of questions 1-5, a model of LSP teacher education and professional development will be provided. We will kindly ask you to provide your thoughts about it.
>
> We look forward to your positive reply and interesting discussion.
>
> Best regards,
>
> Dr Joanna Kic-Drgas
>
> Adam Mickiewicz University, Poland
>
> Dr Violeta Jurkovič
>
> University of Ljubljana, Slovenia

Figure 18. Interview protocol

5.3.3. Data analysis

First, all interviews were automatically transcribed using speech-to-text technology available in Microsoft 365. After the automatic transcription, the written transcripts were manually reviewed and the recordings listened to again in order to identify and correct any inaccuracies or errors introduced during the automatic transcription process. Once accurate transcripts were obtained, machine translation tools were employed to translate the transcriptions from Polish and Slovene into English. The machine-translated versions were then checked again to ensure the accuracy of the translations and identify any inconsistencies or mistranslations that may have occurred during the machine translation process.

Two-stage content analysis of interview transcripts was then used. First, data were read a multitude of times to familiarise with the salient aspects that the interview protocol addressed. Then, the transcripts were coded. In this way, the data were broken into a more manageable form, which allowed common themes and concepts to emerge. To guarantee the anonymity of the participants, their comments were labelled "Pol" for the Polish interviewees and "Slo" for the Slovene interviewees. In the following section, the results of data analysis for each research question will be presented.

5.4. Results

5.4.1. Similarities and differences in the pre-service education of LGP and LSP teachers

Our first research question concerns the similarities and differences between the pre-service education of future LGP teachers and future LSP teachers explored through the responses of the interviewed foreign language teacher educators. The analysis revealed two significant similarities or points in common, which are foreign language proficiency and a solid understanding of foreign language teaching methodology. On the other hand, the main differences concern the knowledge that will be required by LSP teachers: of the target discipline, of language use in the target discipline, of discipline-specific teaching methodology, of needs analysis and needs-based course design, and of materials adaptation and design. The similarities and differences identified are first presented in Figure 19, and then discussed in detail through the application of typical quotations from the interviews.

First of all, the consensus among the interviewees lies in the recognition that foreign language proficiency is a fundamental requirement for anyone aspiring to teach a foreign language, whether within the LGP or LSP domain. Therefore, mastering the target language is seen as a crucial starting point for effective language teaching: *"The similarities are certainly that everybody has to, of course, first of all, focus on language. They have to master the foreign language that they want to teach."* (Slo2)

The second need that both groups of future foreign language teachers share is that they should all first have a solid understanding of how to teach a foreign language: *"I think that a specialised language teacher or a future specialised language teacher is or should be a general language teacher as well, or maybe first*

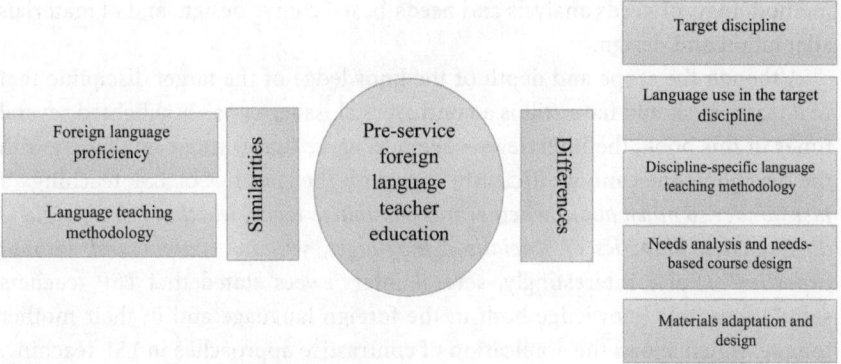

Figure 19. Similarities and differences in the pre-service education of LGP and LSP teachers

of all? First of all, you have to have an understanding of how to teach general language in order to be able to move on to teaching a specialised language." (Pol2)

There are several aspects of foreign language teaching that both groups of teachers need to have a solid base in. A comprehensive description was provided by Slo1: *"So, the common ones are developing comprehension, the whole package, the set of pre, while, post, which goes together with understanding texts, teaching vocabulary, general things, teaching grammar, developing productive competences, that is to say, oral and written communication, because that is relevant in some cases of the foreign languages for specific purposes where, of course, the aim is also productive competence. General things would also be testing and assessment. And planning. I would like to link planning to needs and things like that, say a little bit of longer-term general planning and, of course, lesson planning, that is to say, planning one lesson or one teaching session."*

In addition to these elements, all foreign language teachers also need to learn about different groups of learners so that their teaching can be adapted to meet their target and learning needs: *"So that through this basic education they learn about the characteristics of different target groups, from the teaching of children to adults, so that when they actually teach, they can understand their learners."* (Slo4)

However, the foreign language teacher educators interviewed were also able to identify numerous differences that may characterise the pre-service education of LSP teachers and that would be necessary to equip them with the competences that they will need in their future careers: *"I think definitely this education should look different. /.../ The base and foundation are common to all. On the other hand, the further into this education process we go, the more their paths will diverge."* (Pol6) These differences are, as mentioned above, the knowledge of the target discipline, of language use in the target discipline, of discipline-specific teaching methodology, of needs analysis and needs-based course design, and of materials adaptation and design.

Although the scope and depth of the knowledge of the target discipline that LSP teachers should have still is a controversial issue, as was highlighted several times in this book, the interviewees seem to agree that without familiarity with the discipline one cannot efficiently cope with the specifics of LSP teaching: "*I just wonder so much about whether it is possible to teach, whether it is possible to do didactics, didactics of specialised languages, without content and without expertise.*" (Pol4) Interestingly, several interviewees stated that LSP teachers should have this knowledge both in the foreign language and in their mother tongue, which allows the application of contrastive approaches in LSP teaching: "*Okay, but in English you do not say it that way, so that you can compare, you know, contrast it. One trivial example, in nursing in Slovene we say 'angina' for a sore throat but in English 'angina' is a heart thing, a heart condition. And that is a big difference, so I think they appreciate it here, if you can contrast, if you know how to use it.*" (Slo5)

Knowledge of language use in the target discipline concerns first and foremost discipline-specific terminology: "*In my opinion, the main skill there is, let us say, the use of this specialist vocabulary in all four skills. So there, in my opinion, sort of more emphasis should be on the specialist language in terms of the vocabulary, in terms of the terminology, in terms of the ability where that vocabulary is used.*" (Pol1) However, this terminology is always embedded in typical genres, which is another salient feature of language use in the target discipline: "*An LSP teacher for me has to be much more prepared for the profession, for the language that they have to teach, and what the characteristics are. Because, for example, if you teach the language of tourism, you have to know the typical genres used in tourism.*" (Slo3) What is significant for the education of LSP teachers is that they will need to upgrade their foreign language competence within the discipline-specific domain while there is no such need for LGP teachers: "*All those future teachers who will later work in one of the general programmes can start their career quite successfully with the language skills they have. This is not true for LSP teachers.*" (Slo5)

As stated above, future LGP and LSP teachers share the need of being competent in the application of different teaching approaches and methods. However, according to the interviewees, the teaching methodology in LSP teaching also has "*a certain additional dimension.*" (Pol4) This additional dimension stems from the communicative situations that their learners are or will be likely to encounter in their professional lives: "*It is essential to show future teachers how to create authentic situations in specific contexts.*" (Slo4)

Moreover, if LGP teaching relies on a balanced and sequenced development of all language skills, future LSP teachers need to be aware that the focus in LSP teaching is primarily placed on the language skills and elements that the learner needs or will need even if these precede the usual acquisition of, for instance, grammatical structures. LSP-specific differences in the teaching of grammar were described by Slo3: "*Let us say, what is different is the use of grammar. Because if I have to teach, say, someone who will work as an art historian or a historian, I have to know that even if he is a beginner in Italian, I have to teach him presente storico and passato prossimo, so that he is able to understand them even if he cannot use them yet.*"

The next elements that the pre-service education of LSP teachers should include are needs analysis and needs-based course design or, in other words, a good understanding of the specific learning needs of the learners but also target needs and communication practices in the future or present workplace of LSP learners: "*Conventional language teaching does not cover a very important issue, namely course construction and needs analysis. That is to say, to some extent, for LSP teachers the scope of methodological training is greater.*" (Pol3)

The different needs usually depend on the LSP learners' disciplinary contexts but also age: "*They are usually adults. They may be older, and then you adapt your approach accordingly. /.../ You have to know how to adapt to learners through these approaches so that everybody has a chance to make progress.*" (Slo2). They might also stem from different pre-existing language ability within the same group: "*The biggest problem at the beginning was to find that middle way, to be able to take into consideration their different background and language knowledge, which really comes, I will say, in a wide range, how to work with it.*" (Slo5)

Another competence that might be more significant for LSP than for LGP teachers concerns materials evaluation, adaptation, and design. The most important reason for this relates to the lack of relevant and/or up-to-date textbooks that would suit the needs of specific groups of LSP learners: "*We have also looked at the literature in particular areas and it is sorely lacking. /.../ No, most teachers have to make the effort themselves to look for several different sources to then put something together.*" (Slo5) This in turn means that they "*need to be very well prepared to continually modify curricula, textbooks, exercises and other educational materials, and to be attentive to the use of authentic materials and to use them in classes at lower levels as well.*" (Pol5)

According to the interviewees, motivation may be less of an issue in the education of LSP teachers as LSP learners are often intrinsically motivated to learn the discipline-specific language because they find it to be professionally relevant: "*Language learning motivation is one example. Here, if you teach adults, they are motivated. Here you do not need to address motivation. That is very interesting to my students too.*" (Slo3)

Last but not least, LSP teachers need to be prepared for continuous adaptation to changing terminology and linguistic developments in their respective fields but also, in some cases, for teaching LSP embedded in different contexts or changing these contexts through their teaching careers. This means that the need for the development of the soft skills of flexibility and continuous adaptation to changing circumstances through self-development seem to be more prominent for them than for LGP teachers: "*Teachers of specialised languages should be very sensitive to specifics of the changing world /…/ because we know very well that we live in a dynamic society, and a certain reflection of this dynamic is precisely the specialised language, in which new words, new names are constantly appearing.*" (Pol5) This may have a direct impact on the pre-service education of LSP teachers in terms of the need for the development of analytical competence: "*The fundamental difference between LSP and LGP teacher education, therefore, lies in their ability to analyse the professional context (linguistically, organisationally, culturally, etc.) as a basis for designing and undertaking teaching activities.*" (Pol7)

5.4.2. Elements of disciplinary knowledge essential for LSP teachers

As the analysis of RQ1 indicated, all interviewees seem to agree that disciplinary knowledge should make part of the knowledge repertoire of LSP teachers. Therefore, in the analysis of their views and thoughts expressed in relation to RQ2, we tried to more clearly identify those elements of disciplinary knowledge that foreign language teacher educators think LSP teachers should have. Overall, there seems to be a consensus that LSP teachers need to balance between expertise in the language that they teach and a good understanding of the field or industry in which that language is used. The elements of the disciplinary knowledge that the LSP teachers should have are first presented in Figure 20, and then discussed in detail through typical and illustrative quotations from the interviews.

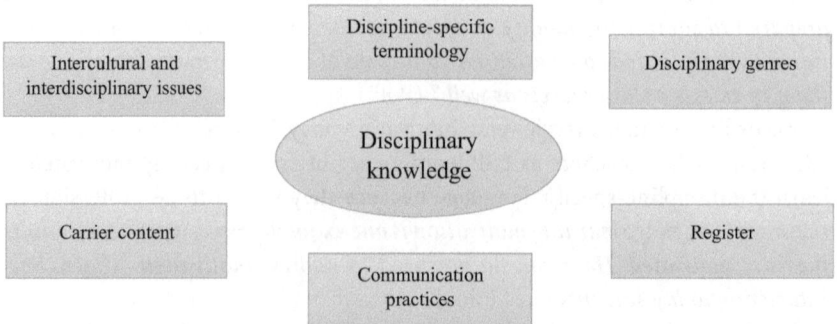

Figure 20. Elements of disciplinary knowledge required by LSP teachers

First of all, most interviewees expressed the view that an LSP teacher should have a solid understanding of discipline-specific terminology, which they need to constantly upgrade and expand to keep pace with the developments in a particular field: "*Every year, hairdressers have new vocabulary, I do not know, what colours are modern, what cuts are modern.*" (Slo5) However, the interviewees are also aware that disciplinary knowledge reaches beyond lexical knowledge: "*It is not only about terminology, that you learn it and then you are ok, it does not work like that.*" (Slo2)

It is generally agreed that LSP teachers should have a solid foundation in disciplinary genres, also as a resource that allows access to discipline-specific terminology: "*I think that for a linguist, and that is what an LSP teacher is, the ability to enter a genre and dissect it, that is to say to dissect professional scientific texts with the right parameters, seems to me to be perhaps a quicker and even more reliable way than through corpora, because corpora produce individual terms across texts.*" (Slo1)

Apart from genres, register, too, understood as the lexical and grammatical choices made by the speaker depending on the situational context, the interlocutors in a conversation, and language function (Halliday, 1989), plays a significant role: "*But yes, of course discourse, just one part of, one aspect of discourse is of course terminology, but there are also other things, there are also structures, there is also the way of communicating, the level of communication, or the register, then the adaptability to different situations.*" (Slo2)

Another salient element of the disciplinary knowledge of LSP teachers is the communication practices relevant to and typical of the discipline that they are teaching, and the knowledge of how that particular professional or scientific community works. Only through the knowledge of the specific communication practices can LSP teachers apply real-life contexts, role-play, and simulations in their LSP teaching. Lack of this knowledge may pose a challenge also to foreign language teacher educators: "*Preparing authentic situations is the biggest challenge for, say, a general language teaching methodologist preparing future teachers for their careers because they simply do not know authentic situations from so many different disciplines.*" (Slo4)

Although LSP teachers may not need to be experts in the specific fields, they should have a general understanding of the industries and subjects related to the language they teach, which in LSP is generally referred to as the carrier content (Dudley-Evans & StJohn, 1998). Most interviewees seem to agree with this point: "*This is essential because if you do not know the profession, then the vocabulary itself means nothing to you. If I just think that I have to translate a set of instructions and I translate them linguistically, the way words are put together, then a mess will come out, which may not even have anything to do with what the instructions actually mean.*" (Slo4)

On the other hand, Pol3 thinks that the level of expertise in the carrier content that an LSP teacher needs depends on the level of mastery of the same content of their learners, i. e., the more experienced the learners are, the less experienced the LSP teacher may be: "*They generally present the view that such subject knowledge is not necessary for the LSP teacher because they work with professionals who are in a sense an equal partner. But in the case of language teachers who work in the early stages of professionalisation /.../, if they are dealing with learners who do not yet have sufficient professional knowledge /.../, so maybe in such a situation they act as an expert not only in terms of language, but also in terms of specialist knowledge.*" The general consensus among the interviewees seems to be that a broad understanding of the field is necessary, while mastery is not: "*I mean, I think certainly an LSP teacher must have a general idea of the industry whose language they have been teaching, a general idea, that is. They simply have to understand what they are talking about but they do not have to be experts in the field, of course.*" (Pol2)

Last but not least, intercultural and interdisciplinary issues may be of importance in several disciplines. This means that LSP teachers should be sensitive to differences between cultures and communication practices in different disciplines or, in other words, the specific communication needs of professionals in different fields, for example nursing: "*In nursing programmes there is a strong emphasis on empathy. Because when you teach a foreign language, you are also teaching a foreign culture, right? So, to do that, you need to have that general knowledge, which is also knowledge of the culture and knowledge of the language.*" (Slo5)

5.4.3. Development of disciplinary knowledge of LSP teachers

The analysis of the interviewees' responses to RQ2 showed that, in their opinion, an LSP teacher should have a broad understanding of the discipline-specific terminology, disciplinary genres and genre analysis, register, communication practices, carrier content, and intercultural and interdisciplinary issues. Therefore, the next aspect that we aimed to explore concerns the opinions of foreign language teacher educators of when and how this broad disciplinary knowledge and understanding should be developed.

Overall, the discussion highlights the importance of integrating discipline-specific education into pre-service language teacher education programmes: "*To some extent, should not that specialised knowledge already start during their studies?*" (Pol4) Otherwise LSP teachers are left to their own resources at the beginning of their careers: "*For me it was just completely new. I never got that from anybody and I had to sort of do it on my own. So, it would be kind of nice /.../ to educate someone in a specialised language."* (Pol1)

However, the interviewees also expressed their opinion that such pre-service LSP teacher education cannot focus on a single discipline because the career path that the students will undertake in their future is unknown: *"So for us, it does not make sense to focus on very specific contexts, it is more about raising awareness, raising awareness of different contexts and different, maybe even slightly different, approaches to teaching."* (Slo2) On the other hand, Slo1 thinks that the use of typical genres from several different disciplines in the pre-service education of LSP teachers should be beneficial to their genre awareness-raising process, which is transferable across disciplines: *"It is possible to connect this with genres, to understand genres, to shake genres from the point of view of terminology or perhaps grammatical structures, to write, to speak, to prepare, to use the texts that are needed /.../ for four or five fields, I would say: natural sciences, technical, social sciences, something in between, which is, let us say, maybe medicine."*

In addition to foreign teacher education courses, other first-cycle or second-cycle degree subjects could be individualised to a certain degree to suit the different interests of future LSP teachers: *"I see more opportunities for this in language subjects, for example language exercises, where a future teacher could, depending on their professional interests, where they would like to be involved later, choose a certain focus. /.../ It would be beneficial to be able to individualise your studies, to be able to choose your field of study in language exercises and to go deeper there, and to be able to access some journals in the field. Maybe some newsletters of companies working in the field you would select."* (Slo2)

Among the interviewees, there seems to be a general consensus that the acquisition of discipline-specific knowledge mostly is achieved through autonomous and self-directed learning of both pre-service as well as in-service LSP teachers. Also at the pre-service stage this could be done by attending LSP conferences: *"We encourage, say, students to attend conferences as helpers, like this student of ours this year."* (Slo5) Another possibility is job shadowing of experienced LSP teachers, which would allow future LSP teachers to familiarise themselves with the specificities of LSP teaching: *"One option might be to do a bit of job shadowing, just to get a feel for what this colleague of yours is actually doing, what this job means."* (Slo4) Self-development at the pre-service stage would be facilitated if future LSP teachers had access to relevant resources: *"Then I would also like to point out that if you want to become an LSP teacher, I think it would be relevant to have access to some literature in this field, let us say, while you are still studying."* (Slo4)

Self-development seems to be the predominant option also for in-service novice LSP teachers, also because at the pre-service stage of education it is very difficult to predict where they would be able to find a job after graduation: *"We do not know where they will get jobs. So, I think the only solution here is to develop this knowledge after they actually get a job, on the job, and start to work intensively on it themselves."* (Slo5) This can mostly be done by consulting various resources, for instance LSP textbooks or materials in the field if they exist: *"I would underline that they can get very good teaching materials from very good LSP teachers. /.../ Because a selection has already been made, it has already been narrowed down to what a very experienced teacher has already found throughout their career to be good, relevant, and useful to teach."* (Slo1) Another option is the use of non-linguistic textbooks designed for students of a particular discipline: *"When I had different disciplines to work with, I basically took a book for that discipline, for example tourism in Italian."* (Slo3) The need for self-development of novice LSP teachers was also described by Pol2: *"They simply learn on the fly, when they get a direction they have never had before, they look for materials themselves, they start to learn the specialist language in question. /.../ They just buy another textbook and study the language themselves, whether they read articles, then they become specialists in that particular field."*

For novice teachers, an option is job shadowing that can take place in the classroom of a more experienced colleague or at a workplace in the target industry: *"If you go to this environment, I think it is the best. /.../ It is one thing to know the theory that somebody gives you. But it is another thing to enter the context itself, and you find out for yourself how and what, then you will be able to more easily pass that on to the students."* (Slo5)

Self-development is not only necessary for novice LSP teachers. While on-the-job, because of the changing circumstances and developing disciplines, experienced LSP teachers need to constantly upgrade their knowledge: *"However, when it comes to professional knowledge, lexical knowledge, the construction of their own offer, they have to be very flexible here and what they received during their studies may not be enough, because what they received during their education was only a response to current needs, which may develop, change and go in an unknown direction."* (Pol5)

5.4.4. Similarities and differences in the continuous professional development of LGP and LSP teachers

As the analysis of RQ3 showed, the development of discipline-specific knowledge of pre-service and in-service LSP teachers usually is self-directed and mostly takes place while on-the-job. As a result, the aim of the next research question was to explore the interviewees' opinions concerning differences and similarities in the continuous professional development of in-service LGP and LSP teachers.

The continuous professional development of LGP teachers and LSP teachers overlaps with regards to competences that both groups of teachers share, for instance language teaching methodology: "*In both cases, teachers keep up to date with new publications, news from the language area, didactic innovations, they improve their linguistic competence and methodological inventory.*" (Pol7) Another common area is the use of ICT. For LSP teachers, this implies following the use of ICT in two domains: "*ICT in teaching and the use of ICT in their discipline.*" (Slo3)

In terms of differences, it is noted that professional development for LSP teachers is less accessible and often requires signing up for specific organisations or courses. In contrast, LGP teachers may have more options for free or certified professional development: "*I can see that the training that is available to teachers of, for example, general language is very often free training, it is certified training, it is training that is accessible to the majority. Specialised language training, on the other hand, is already for a narrower group. /…/ It is not like they are available on the market just like that.*" (Pol1) This may result in a relative isolation of an LSP teacher: "*In short, at this point such a teacher has very little institutional support in terms of courses and it also seems to me that they have relatively little support in terms of exchanging opinions with other teachers in a similar situation.*" (Pol3) In addition, LSP teachers of more widely taught LSPs, such as Business English or languages in tourism, seem to have more professional development opportunities than their peers covering niche LSPs: "*Very often, they need to acquire knowledge of rarer professional languages than the aforementioned language of economics or tourism on their own, and then they develop and improve on their own.*" (Pol3)

This means that LSP teachers often need to engage in self-development activities to keep up with changes and developments in their fields, improve their linguistic competence, and stay up to date with new publications and innovations: "*In the case of LSP teachers, I have the impression that the offer of training for professional development is less accessible and LSP teachers undertake self-development activities on their own and on their own, without being able to count on forms of organised support.*" (Pol7)

Conferences seem to be one of the most highly valued ways for LSP teachers to engage in continuous professional development. These can be LSP conferences that may bring together LSP teachers from different disciplines: "*Because it seems to me that even if we are from different disciplines, it seems to me that you can get ideas and then you move on with colleagues in a way.*" (Slo5) but also discipline-specific conferences dedicated to experts in that particular field: "*To have the opportunity to be informed about developments in the profession. Perhaps by hosting some experts in the field, with the possibility of attending a conference where products or developments in the profession are presented.*" (Slo4) In addition to conferences, continuous professional development may entail visiting or job shadowing professionals working in that particular discipline: "*I would say, well, creating some kind of professional course, professional training, where you can involve these people from the industry and where they will let themselves be involved, well, that would be the optimal solution.*" (Pol2)

LSP teachers' associations seem to play a significant role in this respect, even if they bring together LSP teachers from different disciplines: "*I would like to mention that I think it is very good that communities are being created, such as an association. They can also be quite informal, where you can share experiences because you share some good practices within the different disciplines, and everybody can benefit from that. /.../ And also, after all, for those who are already very experienced, to get some new wind, some new energy.*" (Slo4)

5.4.5. Role of collaboration in the education and professional development of LSP teachers

The last research question addresses the role of collaboration in the pre-service education and in-service professional development of LSP teachers. In general, all interviewees emphasise the importance of collaboration, mentoring, and practical experiences to enhance the quality and relevance of LSP teaching in different fields. The participants in the educational and professional contexts that future or present LSP teachers can collaborate with are presented in Figure 21, and discussed in detail through typical and illustrative quotations from the interviews.

First of all, both pre-service and in-service LSP teachers can enter different forms of collaboration with their peers. For pre-service LSP teachers this most often means collaboration with their fellow students. However, cooperation may also be established between pre-service LSP teachers and students of other disciplines: "*It would be interesting /.../ to create an exchange, say with a profession, to get to know the students who are studying, let us say medicine or nursing.*" (Slo3) An optional element could be completing obligatory teaching practice in LSP contexts which would establish collaboration between pre-service and in-service LSP teachers: "*It would seem to me that the ideal solution would be for them to, for those that would wish to do so, to do the compulsory teaching practice with LSP teachers. /.../ The optimal solution would be mentoring schools.*" (Slo4)

For novice LSP teachers, forms of collaboration with more experienced colleagues may include co-authorship of research papers (Slo3: "*You might invite them to write a paper together with you.*"), classroom observation (Slo1: "*I think that such education also involves observing good LSP teachers.*"), mentoring (Pol3: "*It seems to me that such mentoring could arise in a situation where we are*

Pre-service	In-service
• Peer collaboration with other students and LSP teachers	• Peer collaboration with other LSP teachers
• Disciplinary professionals	• Disciplinary professionals
• General language teaching methodology experts	• General language teaching methodology experts
• Authors of books and other resources	• Authors of books and other resources
	• Disciplinary teachers
	• LSP learners
	• Policy-makers

Figure 21. Collaboration opportunities for pre-service and in-service LSP teachers

talking about teachers who teach popular specialised languages economics, tourism, medicine, etc. /.../ And a situation where a mentor and a young teacher who is learning, all their experiences meet. Such situations are likely to occur in language centres, for example, where there are more LSP teachers."), and sharing teaching materials (Slo5: *"I got them from a colleague who already had them put together."*).

Finally, for experienced in-service LSP teachers, collaboration with their peers means collaboration with other LSP teachers. The most frequent meeting points mentioned by the interviewees are LSP conferences: *"Maybe conferences such as ours. I think this is very, very welcome."* (Slo5), and national and international associations: *"And I do not know how this should be organised, whether it should be within the framework of some kind of project, whether there should be some kind of, I do not know, Association of Academic Teachers of Specialised Language, some kind of place, probably virtual these days, where you could meet or add some material, ask questions, where there would be some kind of forum, a place where you could exchange experience, and learn from each other. /.../ I think this is the perfect time to just start working on collaborations that could be not just national collaborations, but international collaborations."* (Pol1)

A different form of collaboration is that with disciplinary professionals who already work in a particular target context. For pre-service LSP teachers, cooperation with disciplinary professionals could be organised within work placement opportunities. This would allow them to develop the disciplinary knowledge not only in a foreign language but also in their mother tongue: *"It would also be very beneficial for students of a foreign language to have the opportunity to do a short internship within a company that is active in that profession, so that they* could hear the language in Slovene and see how it is used, because this is language that they would not normally use or know even in their mother language." (Slo4) For in-service LSP teachers, on the other hand, cooperation with disciplinary professionals would provide invaluable data to the needs analysis process: *"However, I would very much like it to be real and realistic to cooperate with, well, people from the industry, so that they would guide a little bit of the needs analysis, so that they would get involved."* (Pol2), and allow LSP teachers to build and upgrade their knowledge of the discipline and communicative practices: *"Or some experts, so that you can do a little observation there, or listen."* (Slo1)

General language teaching methodology experts are shareholders that both pre-service and in-service LSP teachers may collaborate with. For the former group, this takes place during their pre-service teacher education programmes while for the latter general language teaching methodology experts may organise professional development opportunity events aiming to upgrade the LSP teachers' foreign language teaching competences: *"Maybe we could provide some workshops for you."* (Slo5) On the other hand, experienced LSP teachers may act as mentors to the pre-service LSP teachers during their teaching practice periods while they are still involved in formal education courses held by general language teaching methodology experts: *"Here I also see one good opportunity for cooperation between us, general language teaching methodology experts and LSP teachers."* (Slo5)

An interesting viewpoint in terms of collaboration opportunities for pre-service and in-service LSP teachers was stated by Slo1 who thinks that relying on any kind of resource, for example printed or audio-visual material, is a form of cooperation with their authors: *"This is essentially collaboration with the general pedagogical skills of the giants on whose shoulders you stand."*

An almost essential form of collaboration for in-service LSP teachers that most interviewees mentioned is collaboration with disciplinary teachers. This may take different formats, such as forms of team-teaching (Slo4: *"Someone who teaches the discipline and someone who teaches the language, so the two of them do joint lessons, maybe split a seminar, some exercises, and can cover both the content and the language."*) that allow the LSP teacher to *"compensate for their own deficiencies in the discipline"* (Pol7). Another interesting way to collaborate with disciplinary teachers is to ask them to evaluate LSP teaching materials to corroborate their validity and provide suggestions: *"Then these materials can be solved and evaluated by teachers of specialist subjects. They might say, gee, it would be nice to do this and this as well. And then you say, where can I find out about that, do you have anything?"* (Slo1). Last but not least, attending classes of disciplinary teachers may be a means to build a novice LSP teacher's disciplinary knowledge: *"And a young LSP teacher should invite themselves to some lessons of the disciplinary teachers. And maybe ask when there is some material that is really essential and attend that class."* (Slo1)

Importantly, in-service LSP teachers may enter different forms of collaboration also with their learners, i.e., students or participants attending the LSP course. This mostly happens as an element of the needs analysis process with LSP learners who already work in a particular professional context: *"They are a very important factor here. This is needs analysis. Just to ask them beforehand what situations they expect to find themselves in, in their professions, the most typical situations, the type of language used there."* (Slo2) In addition, the LSP learners may act as providers or authentic materials: *"Yes, the participants also gave me the materials. And if I was in the classroom, I would ask them to give me the same if they have any. Some special thing, let us say, that they wanted to work on. Because then it is easy to collaborate, because you as a language teacher can help them, but they can help you as well. This is collaborative learning."* (Slo3)

A last, but by no means less significant form of collaboration is that between the LSP teaching community and the policy-makers, who decide how, when, and how much LSP teaching will be done, especially in formal education settings: *"I see a great need for all those involved in the LSP learning process to work together, not only teachers and students, but also educational policy-makers (especially if LSP learning is part of formal education) or employers. Through such wide-ranging collaboration, the teacher learns about the needs/expectations of the principals and beneficiaries of education, who should not in every situation be equated with the learners themselves, gets to know and better understand the professional context, has the opportunity to obtain authentic materials, and to verify the effectiveness of their teaching activities."* (Pol7)

5.5. Synthesis

As mentioned in the Introduction, the objective of the analysis presented in this chapter was to explore the views of foreign language teacher educators on the pre-service education and in-service professional development of LSP teachers in order to complement the picture on LSP teacher education and professional development painted by previous studies that relied on LSP teachers as respondents in quantitative studies and interviewees in qualitative studies.

The findings of the qualitative analysis of the semi-structured interviews provided in this chapter mostly corroborate the findings of previous studies. This means that LSP teachers and foreign language teacher educators share the same views on a number of aspects related to LSP teacher education and professional development in general. For instance, they agree that a general language teaching methodology course provides solid foundations for LGP and LSP teachers, but also that the additional competences that LSP teachers need to develop should be addressed in a separate, additional course. The fact that – on the contrary – research revealed that the pre-service LSP teacher education programmes in the EHEA that do exist are far from being standardised (Bocanegra-Valle & Perea-Barberá, 2023; John et al., 2023) further strengthens the importance of the role of policy-makers, which was emphasised by one of the interviewees. The gap in the provision of programmes that would consolidate the necessary additional skills and competences of LSP teachers can now, at least partly, be bridged by self-directed engagement in online courses developed within the Catapult and LSP-TEOC.Pro courses. The LSP-TEOC.Pro OER especially was built on the notion of the LSP teacher as a ""reflective practitioner" – someone who reflects on the practice of their profession as a way of developing expertise in it." (Burazer & Skela, 2023, p. 8)

Next, LSP teachers and foreign language teacher educators also agree that an LSP teacher should have a broad range of knowledge in relation to the target discipline, including knowledge of the discipline (or carrier content) itself. However, the development of the required level of expertise is generally left to the autonomous and self-directed efforts of the LSP teachers when they start their LSP teaching careers. Nevertheless, it must be pointed out that the interviewed foreign language teacher educators are undoubtedly aware that awareness-raising of typical genres in the discipline, communicative situations, and discipline-specific terminology should start already at the pre-service LSP teacher education stage. This again refers to the importance of policy-makers at the governmental levels as well as levels of individual universities because the required awareness of the discipline cannot be appropriately addressed if no specific LSP teacher education programmes exist.

Another feature that emerged from these interviews but was only sporadically addressed in previous research studies, for example by Bocanegra-Valle and Perea-Barberá (2023), is the increasing need for the development of soft or transversal skills, also, or in particular among LSP teachers. In fact, it seems that flexibility, the ability to engage in self-directed and autonomous learning, and intercultural skills are transversal skills might characterise LSP teachers more typically than other groups of foreign language teachers.

The results of this study indicate the high value that foreign language teacher educators ascribe to collaboration at various stages of an LSP teacher's career. This, however, only in part resonates with the findings of Jurkovič et al. (2023), namely that the only core professional development need that referred to peer collaboration seems to be engagement in LSP communities of practice, which usually occurs by attending LSP conferences. Therefore, various forms of collaboration among different stakeholders might be an avenue that the LSP teaching community should strengthen and consolidate in the future, also to assist novice LSP teachers at the beginning of their careers (see Podgoršek et al., 2021).

Last but not least, previous research showed that continuous professional development is not a priority for all LSP teachers (Bocanegra-Valle and Perea-Barberá, 2023; Jurkovič et al., 2023). A question that the LSP teaching community would have to answer in this case concerns the causal relationship between the scarce offer of suitable professional development opportunities on the one hand and professional development opportunities as a need that is not at the core of an LSP teacher on the other hand. Are there few professional development opportunities tailored to LSP teachers because there is a lower-than-expected interest in these opportunities among LSP teachers? Or, alternatively, does the lower-than-expected interest stem from the absence of relevant opportunities? Undoubtedly, a significant factor is the high specialisation level of many LSP teachers, in many niche disciplines that would be difficult to put into a common denominator.

Conclusion

Every reader is encouraged to derive their own personalised insights, drawing connections to their unique professional and personal situations while engaging with the content of this book. Before exploring the summaries and takeaways we have provided in the following paragraphs, one for each major chapter, the readers might take a moment to reflect on their own personal takeaways. In this way, we aim to enhance the applicability of the book's concepts to diverse geographical, personal, professional, educational, and other contexts.

The first major chapter, titled Context, as its title implies, presents the context of the education, professional development, and work in two EU countries, Poland and Slovenia, with similar and yet different LSP circumstances and conditions, essentially engendered by the national legislation and therefore policymakers. Therefore, despite the current parallel political situation in Poland and Slovenia and the resulting similarities, their educational systems, linguistic contexts, and language policies display some important differences, which may also influence the education, professional development, status and work conditions of LSP teachers. This indicates the importance of addressing LSP teacher education and professional development issues both at the national as well as international level.

The Introduction to LSP provides a clear definition of LSP by comparing it with, and distinguishing it from related concepts. Importantly, this chapter provides fundamental insights into the key concepts that LSP is built on: needs analysis, curriculum and syllabus design, materials design, teaching methodology, and assessment. LSP teaching is related but also essentially different from related concepts such as EMI and CLIL. As a result, knowledge in some of the fundamental LSP issues may be transferable to other contexts that integrate content and language teaching, for instance, materials design in LSP and CLIL may follow inherently similar processes and result in similar products. On the other hand, knowledge in other fundamental LSP issues may be less transferable, for instance, the target and learning needs of learners in EMI contexts would be significantly different from those in LSP contexts.

LSP Teachers is a chapter entirely dedicated to LSP teachers as a frequently overlooked stakeholder in the LSP teaching and learning context. This is why it discusses the intertwining concepts of LSP teacher roles, competences, identity, challenges, and communities of practice; the latter may play a defining role in the professional growth of any LSP teacher. Because of the variety of demanding roles that LSP teachers play and the complex competences that they need to develop, international communities of practice may play an essential role in the professional development of LSP teachers. International networking and support appears even more important for LSP teachers of less widely taught languages and niche disciplines who may not have any LSP peers in their own institutional or even national contexts.

LSP Teacher Professional Development Projects is a chapter that presents three Erasmus+ projects recently funded by the European Commission: TRAILS, Catapult, and LSP-TEOC.Pro. The results of these projects have not only made a significant contribution to LSP teacher development and its research. They have also increased the visibility of the LSP community of practice and corroborated the support of the EU policy-makers. International projects may have a number of beneficial effects on the international community of practice of LSP teachers. First of all, they produce results that can help LSP teachers develop their LSP teaching competences through self-directed learning and thus compensate for the absence of standardised LSP teacher education and professional development programmes. No less importantly, they provide opportunities for the creation of international networks of LSP teachers and further synergy effects realised through other forms of collaboration, such as co-authorship, attendance and organisation of conferences, mentoring and exchange of good practices, to name just a few.

The fifth major chapter, titled LSP Teacher Education and Professional Development, brings previously unpublished results of a qualitative study conducted by means of semi-structured interviews with foreign language teacher educators as important stakeholders in the education and professional development of all foreign language teachers. In this way, it contributes to a holistic picture of LSP teacher education and development, and complements the results of previous studies in this field in which data were provided by LSP teachers themselves. Importantly, LSP teachers and foreign language teacher educators share the same views on a number of aspects related to LSP teacher education and professional development. Among these, there is an awareness of the importance of genres and genre analysis competences, which allow LSP teachers to have an insight into the target needs of their learners but also access to relevant discipline-specific terminology and thus language use in the target discipline.

The journey embarked upon within the pages of this book started with an invitation to revisit already known, or to discover new paths in the field of LSP teacher education and professional development. In the same manner, it will close with an open-ended invitation to continue charting new personal and professional paths in the LSP domain through LSP teaching, research, and projects. The latter open up a number of opportunities for international and intercultural cooperation among LSP teachers and learners. Here we will name just three: the critical use of AI in LSP teaching, banks of LSP materials for learners in different disciplines and at different levels of language competence, and apps designed for LSP teachers looking for matching LSP colleagues in other countries. Hopefully, in a few years we will be able to read about them in a book similar to this one.

List of tables

Table 1:	Legislative documents that regulate the educational system in Poland	17
Table 2:	LSP provision for students of first-cycle and second-cycle degree studies at the Faculty of Modern Languages and Literature at Adam Mickiewicz university	25
Table 3:	Legislative documents that regulate the educational system in Slovenia	31–32
Table 4:	LSP provision at the Faculty of Maritime Studies and Transport of the University of Ljubljana (Maritime Department)	40
Table 5:	LSP provision at the Faculty of Maritime Studies and Transport of the University of Ljubljana (Transport Technology Department)	40
Table 6:	List of factors and their influence on a curriculum	56
Table 7:	Differences between curriculum and syllabus (see Basturkmen, 2010)	59
Table 8:	Purpose of assessment (see Northern Illinois University Center for Innovative Teaching and Learning (2012); Anthony, 2018)	66–67
Table 9:	LSP teacher identity (Mahendra, 2020) based on the practice-centred frames of teacher identity (Pennington, 2015)	81–82
Table 10:	Description of TRAILS intellectual outputs (IOs)	92
Table 11:	Core professional development needs of LSP teachers and consensus rate among survey respondents (Jurkovič et al., 2023; see also Bocanegra-Valle & Perea-Barbera, 2023)	93–94
Table 12:	Description of Catapult IOs	96–97
Table 13:	Description of LSP-TEOC.PRO intellectual outputs (IOs)	99–100

List of figures

Figure 1:	Primary education in Poland (see Grzelak & Roszko-Wójtkowicz, 2017)	18
Figure 2:	Secondary education in Poland (see Grzelak & Roszko-Wójtkowicz, 2017)	19
Figure 3:	Higher education in Poland (see Grzelak & Roszko-Wójtkowicz, 2017)	20
Figure 4:	Pillars of teaching languages for specific purposes (Sowa, 2015)	23
Figure 5:	Syllabus of the LSP teaching course at Adam Mickiewicz University in Poznań, Poland	28–29
Figure 6:	Structure of the education system in Slovenia (for details, see the Slovene Education System and Slovene Qualifications Framework)	33
Figure 7:	EMI, CLIL, and LSP placed on a continuum of programmes that integrate content and language (adapted from Thompson & McKinley, 2018)	50
Figure 8:	Four pillars of LSP (Anthony, 2018)	51
Figure 9:	Cycle of needs analysis integration into a course (see Flowerdew, 2013, p. 325)	54
Figure 10:	Steps of LSP curriculum design (see Basturkmen, 2010; Sowa, 2022a, 2022b)	58
Figure 11:	Features of efficient LSP materials based on Krzanowski (1998)	61
Figure 12:	Stages of task-based learning (see Atabekova, 2009)	64
Figure 13:	Key professional identities of LSP teachers (Chang, 2017)	81
Figure 14:	6-pillar model of LSP teacher education and professional development	94
Figure 15:	TRAILS curriculum (TRAILS, 2021)	95
Figure 16:	Content of online course LSP-TEOC.Pro	101
Figure 17:	Professional development needs of LSP teachers (Bocanegra-Valle & Basturkmen, 2019)	109
Figure 18:	Interview protocol	115
Figure 19:	Similarities and differences in the pre-service education of LGP and LSP teachers	117
Figure 20:	Elements of disciplinary knowledge required by LSP teachers	120
Figure 21:	Collaboration opportunities for pre-service and in-service LSP teachers	127

References

Abedeen, F. (2015). *Exploration of ESP teacher knowledge and practices at tertiary and applied colleges in Kuwait: Implications for pre- and in-service ESP teacher training.* Exeter. https://ore.exeter.ac.uk/repository/bitstream/handle/10871/17437/AbedeenF.pdf?sequence=1.

Ali, S. U. (2015). ESP teacher education model in Indonesian context. *EDUKASI Jurnal Pendidikan, 13*(2), 344–354.

Almabekova, O. A. (2010). Reflective Teaching in ESP. *Journal of Siberian Federal University, Humanities & Social Sciences 3*(3), 462–475.

Alsharif, D., & Shukri, N. (2018). Exploring pedagogical challenges of ESP teachers at a Saudi Arabian university. *International Journal of Asian Social Science, 8*(10), 841–855. https://doi.org/10.18488/journal.1.2018.810.841.855.

Anesa, P., & Deyrich, M–C. (2023). Responding to LSP teacher needs: evolving challenges and new paradigms. In M-A. Chateaureynaud and P. John (Eds.), *LSP Teacher Training Summer School. The TRAILs Project* (97–110). Peter Lang.

Anthony, L. (2018). *Introducing English for Specific Purposes*. Routledge.

Atabekova, A. (2009) Task-based LSP learning with concordance and cognition technologies, *EDULEARN09 Proceedings*, 4421–4425.

Bachman, L.F., & Palmer, A.S. (1996). *Language Testing in Practice: Designing and Developing Useful Language Tests*. Oxford University Press.

Bajerowska, A. (2013). *Sposoby transferencji wiedzy specjalistycznej.* https://depotuw.ceon.pl/bitstream/handle/item/704/Bajerowska_doktorat.pdf?sequence=1.

BALEAP. (2008). *Competency Framework for Teachers of English for Academic Purposes.* https://www.baleap.org/wp-content/uploads/2016/04/teap-competency-framework.pdf.

Barwell, R. (2005). Critical issues for language and content in mainstream classroom. *Linguistics and Education, 16*(2), 143–150. https://doi.org/10.1016/j.linged.2006.01.003.

Basturkmen, H. (2010). *Developing courses in English for specific purposes*. Palgrave Macmillan.

Basturkmen, H. (2014). LSP teacher education: Review of literature and suggestions for the research agenda. *Iberica, 28,* 17–34.

Basturkmen, H., & Elder, C. (2004). The practice of LSP. In A. Davies and C. Elder (Eds.), *The Handbook of Applied Linguistics* (pp. 672–694). Blackwell Publishing Ltd. https://doi.org/10.1002/9780470757000.ch27.

Basturkmen, H., & Bocanegra-Valle, A. (2018). Materials design processes, beliefs and practices of experienced ESP teachers in university settings in Spain. In Y. Kırkgöz and K. Dikilitaş (Eds.), *Key Issues in English for Specific Purposes in Higher Education* (pp. 13–27). Springer. Belcher, D. (2009). What ESP is and can be: an introduction. In D. Belcher (Ed.), *English for Specific Purposes in Theory and Practice* (pp. 1–20). University of Michigan Press.

Belcher, D. (2013). The future of ESP research: resources for access and choice. In B. Paltridge and S. Starfield (Eds.), *The Handbook of English for Specific Purposes* (pp. 535–551). Wiley-Blackwell.

Berdychowska, Z. (2010). Komunikacja specjalistyczna na studiach filologicznych: podstawy lingwistyczne i profile kompetencyjne. *Lingwistyka stosowana, 3*, 61–70.

Blumenfeld, P., Fishman, B.J., Krajcik, J., Marx, R.W., & Soloway, E. (2000). Creating usable innovations in systemic reform: scaling up technology-embedded project-based science in urban schools. *Educational Psychologist, 35*(3), 149–164. https://doi.org/10.1207/S15326985EP3503_2.

Bocanegra Valle, A. (2012). El profesor de inglés para fines específicos ante el Espacio Europeo de Educación Superior. *Aula, 18*, 29–41. https://doi.org/10.14201/8870.

Bocanegra-Valle, A. (2016). Needs analysis for curriculum design. In K. Hyland and P. Shaw (Eds.), *The Routledge Handbook of English for Academic Purposes* (pp. 560–576). Routledge.

Bocanegra-Valle, A. & Perea-Barbera, L. (2023). A quantitative analysis of LSP teacher needs across the European Higher Education Area. In M-A. Chateaureynaud & P. John (Eds.), *LSP Teacher Training Summer School. The TRAILs Project* (pp. 111–130). Peter Lang.

Bocanegra-Valle, A., & Basturkmen, H. (2019). Investigating the teacher education needs of experienced ESP teachers in Spanish universities. *Ibérica, 38*, 127–149.

Brown, J. D. (1989). Language program evaluation: A synthesis of existing possibilities. In K. Johnson (Ed.), *The Second Language Curriculum* (pp. 222–241). Cambridge University Press.

Brown, J. D. (2016). *Introducing Needs Analysis and English for Specific Purposes.* Routledge.

Burazer, L., & Skela, J. (2023). Foreword. In J. Skela and L. Burazer, *Teacher Development Resource Book for Pre-service ELT Education Programs* (pp. 7–8). Tangram.

Celinšek, D., & Bobanović, M. (2022). Tutorship and student autonomy in teamwork and problem-solving in LSP teaching. *Scripta Manent, 17*(1), 29–50.

Chang, C-W. (2014) Teachers' beliefs and practices about ESP assessment: a phenomenographic study. *The Journal of Teaching English for Specific and Academic Purposes, 2*(4), 625–645.

Chang, K. C. (2017). From EAP to ESP: teacher's identity development. *Taiwan Journal of TESOL, 14*(2), 71–100.

Charles, M., & Pecorari, D. (2016). *Introducing English for Academic Purposes.* Routledge.

Chateaureynaud, M-A., & John, P. (Eds.)(2023). *LSP Teacher Training Summer School. The TRAILs Project.* Peter Lang.

Chen, T-Y. (2000). Self-training for ESP through action research. *English for Specific Purposes, 19*, 389–402.

References

Chen, M., Flowerdew, J., & Anthony, L. (2019). Introducing in-service English language teachers to datadriven learning for academic writing. *System*, 87, 102–148. https://doi.org/10.1016/j.system.2019.102148.

Cocco, S. (2006). *Student Leadership Development: the Contribution of Project-based Learning*. Royal Roads University. https://central.bac-lac.gc.ca/.item?id=MR17869&op=pdf&app=Library&oclc_number=271429340.

Cole, C., Pritchard, B., & Trenkner, P. (2007). Maritime English instruction – ensuring instructors' competence. *Ibérica*, 14, 123–147.

Čuk, J. (2015). *Slovenščina: južnoslovanski jezik, ki ga na svetu govori približno 2,5 milijona govorcev*. Statistical Office of the Republic of Slovenia. https://www.stat.si/statweb/News/Index/5004.

Dearden, J. (2014). *English as a medium of instruction – a growing global phenomenon*. British Council.

Ding, A., & Campion, G. (2016). EAP teacher development. In K. Hyland and P. Shaw (Eds.), *The Routledge Handbook of English for Academic Purposes* (pp. 547–559). Routledge.

Djurić, M. (1999). Kako lahko preoblikujemo tradicijo ESP/EAP v Sloveniji: dodiplomska stopnja. *Vestnik Društva za tuje jezike in književnosti Slovenije*, 33(1–2), 7–22.

Douglas, D. (2000). *Assessing Language for Specific Purposes*. Cambridge University Press.

Duch, B. J., Groh, S. E., & Allen, D. E. (2001). Why problem-based learning? A case study of institutional change in undergraduate education. In B. Duch, S. Groh and D. Allen (Eds.), *The Power of Problem-based Learning* (pp.3–11). Stylus.

Dudley-Evans, T. (2001). English for specific purposes. In R. Carter and D. Nunan (Eds.), *The Cambridge Guide to Teaching English to Speakers of Other Languages* (pp. 131–136). Cambridge University Press.

Dudley-Evans, T., & StJohn, M.J. (1998). *Developments in English for specific purposes*. Cambridge University Press.

Dudzik, A., Dzięcioł-Pędich, A., & Kic-Drgas, J. (2019). ESP testing in the eyes of Polish tertiary teachers. *Linguodidactica* XXIII, 21–35.

Duyen, L. T. H. (2014). Learning to teach ESP: case studies of two Vietnamese general English teachers. *Language Education in Asia*, 5(2), 228–237. http://dx.doi.org/10.5746/LEiA/14/V5/I2/A05/Duyen.

Early, P. (1981). The ESP teacher's role – implications for the 'knower-client' relationship. In *The ESP Teacher: Role, Development and Prospects. ELT Documents 112* (pp. 42–52). British Council.

Ellis, R. (2009). Task-based language teaching: sorting out the misunderstandings. *International Journal of Applied Linguistics*, 19(3), 221–246. https://doi.org/10.1111/j.1473-4192.2009.00231.x.

Eurydice. (2018). *The System of Education in Poland*. https://eurydice.eacea.ec.europa.eu/national-education-systems/poland/organisation-education-system-and-its-structure.

European Commission. (2017). *Communication from the Commission to the European Parliament, the Council, the European Economic and Social Committee and the Committee of the Regions*. https://eur-lex.europa.eu/legal-content/EN/TXT/PDF/?uri=CELEX:52017DC0247&from=DA.

Ewer, J. R. (1983). Teacher training for EST: problems and methods. *The ESP Journal*, 2, 9–31.

Flowerdew, L. (2013). Needs analysis and curriculum development. In B. Paltridge and S. Starfield (Eds.), *The Handbook of English for Specific Purposes* (pp. 325-346). John Wiley and Sons. https://doi.org/10.1002/9781118339855.ch17.

Gajewska, E. (2022). Preparing a philologist for specialised communication: LSP and specialised translation. In J. Kic-Drgas and J. Woźniak (Eds.), *Perspectives on LSP Teacher Training in Poland* (pp. 58-111). FRSE Publishing. https://doi.org/10.47050/6 6515796.

Gajewska, E., & Sowa, M. (2015). Sposoby kształcenia nauczycieli języków specjalistycznych: od rzeczywistości edukacyjnej do rozwiązań systemowych, *Neofilolog*, (44)2, 221-235.

Gajewska, E., Sowa, M., & Kic-Drgas, J. (2020). *Filologia wobec wyzwań komunikacji specjalistycznej: od współpracy z biznesem po kształcenie nauczycieli*. Wydawnictwo UAM.

Geiger, S., Dombois, C., & Funke, J. (2018). The role of environmental knowledge and attitude: predictors for ecological behavior across cultures? An analysis of Argentinean and German students. *Umweltpsychologie, 22*(1), 69-87.

Grosse, C.U., & Voght, G. M. (2012). The continuing evolution of languages for specific purposes. *The Modern Language Journal*, 96, 190-202. https://doi.org/10.1111/j.1540-4781.2012.01304.x.

Grucza, S. (2013). *Od lingwistyki tekstów do lingwistyki języków specjalistycznych*. Wydawnictwo Naukowe Instytutu Kulturologii i Lingwistyki Antropocentrycznej, Uniwersytet Warszawski.

Grzelak, M. M., & Roszko-Wójtowicz, E. (2017) System Edukacji w Polsce - wybrane problemy. *Myśl Ekonomiczna i Polityczna, 2*(57), 275-305.

Hall, J. D. (2011). *Self-Directed Learning Characteristics of First-Generation, First-Year College Students Participating in a Summer Bridge Program*. University of South Florida. https://digitalcommons.usf.edu/etd/3140/.

Halliday, M. A. K. (1989). *Spoken and Written Language*. Oxford University Press.

Hmelo-Silver, C.E. (2004). Problem-based learning. What and how do students learn. *Educational Psychology Review, 16*, 235--266. https://doi.org/10.1023/B:EDPR.0000034 022.16470.f3.

Huhta, M., Vogt, K., Johnson, E., & Tulkki, H. (2013). *Needs Analysis for Language Course Design. A Holistic Approach to ESP*. Cambridge University Press.

Hulstijn, J. H. (2003). Incidental and intentional learning. In C. J. Doughty and M. H. Long (Eds.), *Handbook of Second Language Acquisition* (pp. 349-381). Blackwell.

Hutchinson, T., & Waters, A. (1987). *English for Specific Purposes. A Learning-centred Approach*. Cambridge University Press.

Hüttner, J., Smit, U., & Mehlmauer-Larcher, B. (2009). ESP teacher education at the interface of theory and practice: Introducing a model of mediated corpus-based genre analysis. *System, 37*, 99-109. https://doi.org/10.1016/j.system.2008.06.003.

Hyland, K.(2002). Genre: Language, context and literacy. *Annual Review of Applied Linguistics, 22*, 113-135.

Hyland, K. (2007). Genre pedagogy: language, literacy and L2 writing instruction. *Journal of Second Language Writing, 16*(3), 148-164. https://doi.org/10.1016/j.jslw.2007.07.005.

Hyland, K. (2016). General and specific EAP. In K. Hyland & P. Shaw (Eds.), *The Routledge Handbook of English for Academic Purposes* (pp. 17-29). Routledge.

International Maritime Organization. (2015). *Model Course 3.17. Maritime English*. International Maritime Organization.
Iswati, L., &Triastuti, A. (2021). Voicing the challenges of ESP teaching: lessons from ESP in non-English departments. *Studies in English Language and Education, 8*(1), 276–293. https://doi.org/10.24815/siele.v8i1.17301.
Jarvis, J. (1983). Two core skills for ESP teachers. *The ESP Journal, 2*(1), 45–48. https://doi.org/10.1016/0272-2380(83)90012-4.
John, P., Greenwood, R., Jurkovič, V., Kereković, S., & Kic-Drgas, J. (2023). Identification and analysis of LSP teacher training programmes in Europe. In M-A. Chateaureynaud and P. John (Eds.), *LSP Teacher Training Summer School. The TRAILs project* (pp. 31–42). Peter Lang.
Jurkovič, V. (Ed.) (2005). *Guide to Problem-based Learning*. Slovene Association of LSP Teachers.
Jurkovič, V. (2019). Online informal learning of English through smartphones in Slovenia. *System, 80*, 27–37. https://doi.org/10.1016/j.system.2018.10.007.
Jurkovič, V., & Djurić, M. (2008). Tuji jeziki stroke v slovenskem visokem šolstvu. In M. Ivšek and L. Aase (Eds.), *Jeziki v izobraževanju: zbornik prispevkov konference* (pp. 215–221). Zavod RS za šolstvo.
Jurkovič, V., Djurić, M., & Godnič Vičič, Š. (2008). Status učitelja tujega jezika stroke v visokem šolstvu. In M. Brkan, Š. Godnič Vičič, M. Jarc, V. Jurkovič and V. Zorko (Eds.), *Inter Alia 1*. http://www.sdutsj.edus.si/InterAlia/index_en.html.
Jurkovič, V., Mertelj, D., & Podgoršek, S. (2023). A further step toward a definition of the core professional development needs of LSP teachers in the EHEA. *RESLA*. In press.
Kayi-Aydar, H. (2019). Language teacher identity. *Language Teaching, 52*(3), 281–295. https://doi.org/10.1017/S0261444819000223.
Kennedy, C., & Bolitho, R. (1984). *English for Specific Purposes*. Macmillan.
Kic-Drgas, J. (2022). *Entwicklung der Schreibkompetenz in einer Fremdsprache an der Hochschule. Konzept für die Schreibvermittlung im berufsbezogenen Unterricht am Beispiel von Deutsch als Fremdsprache*. Vandenhoeck & Ruprecht.
Kic- Drgas, J., & Woźniak, J. (2020). Fachsprachendidaktik an europäischen Hochschulen – Stand und Perspektiven In S. Adamczak-Krysztofowicz, A. Szczepaniak-Kozak and P. Rybszleger (Hg.), *Angewandte Linguistik. Neue Herausforderungen und Konzepte* (S. 311–331). Vandenhoeck & Ruprecht Verlage.
Kic-Drgas, J., & Woźniak, J. (Eds.). (2022a). *Perspectives on LSP Teacher Training in Poland*. FRSE Publishing. https://doi.org/10.47050/66515796.
Kic-Drgas, J., & Woźniak, J. (2022b). Projekt TRAILs jako odpowiedź na potrzeby w zakresie kształcenia nauczycieli języków specjalistycznych. In J. Kic-Drgas and J. Woźniak (Eds.), *Perspectives on LSP Teacher Training in Poland* (pp. 116–136). FRSE Publishing. https://doi.org/10.47050/66515796.
Kirkgöz, Y. (2019). ESP in teacher education: a case study. In S. Papadima-Sophocleous, E. Kakoulli Constantinou and C. N. Giannikas (Eds.), *ESP Teaching and Teacher Education: Current Theories and Practices* (pp. 13–26). Research-publishing-net. https://doi.org/10.14705/rpnet.2019.33.923.
Kirkgöz, Y, & Dikilitaş, K. (Eds.). (2018). *Key Issues in English for Specific Purposes in Higher Education*. Springer.

Kilickaya F., & Kic-Drgas, J. (2020). Issues of context and design in OER (open educational resources). *Educational Technology Research and Development*, *69*, 401–405.

Klimova, B. (2015). Developing ESP study materials for students at a non-philological faculty. *Procedia – Social and Behavioral Sciences*, *197*, 104–107. https://doi.org/10.1016/j.sbspro.2015.07.063.

Krajka, J. (2018). The ESP teacher as a researcher – from needs analysis to materials development. *Scripta Manent*, *13*, 2–25.

Krzanowski, M. (1998). *Materials design in teaching English for Academic Purposes (EAP)*. Paper presented at the 32nd IATEFL Annual International Conference, UMIST, Manchester, 14–18 April.

Lambert, C. (2010). A task-based needs analysis: putting principles into practice. *Language Teaching Research*, *14*(1), 99–112. https://doi.org/10.1177/1362168809346520.

Li, B. (2022). Perceptions of ESP lecturers' professional development in China: an ecological perspective. *Journal of Education and Learning*, *11*(4), 92–102. https://doi.org/10.5539/jel.v11n4p92.

Lopes, J. B., & Cunha, A. E. (2017). Self-directed professional development to improve effective teaching: key points for a model. *Teaching and Teacher Education*, *68*, 262–274. https://doi.org/10.1016/j.tate.2017.09.009.

López-Zurita, P., & Vázquez-Amador, M. (2023). A qualitative analysis of LSP teacher needs across the European Higher Education Area. In M-A. Chateaureynaud & P. John (Eds.), *LSP Teacher Training Summer School. The TRAILs Project* (pp. 131–152). Peter Lang.

Mahendra, A. W. (2020). Constructing identity: experiences of Indonesian ESP teachers in a language institute. *English Language Teaching Educational Journal*, *3*(3), 229–240. https://doi.org/10.12928/eltej.v3i3.2560.

Maleki, A. (2008). ESP teaching: a matter of controversy. *ESP World*, *1*(17), 1–21.

Marjanovikj-Apostolovski, M., & Macedonia, N. (2019). Developing teaching materials for ESP courses: the last option many ESP teachers resort to. *SEEU Review*, *14*(2), 160–177. https://doi.org/10.2478/seeur-2019-0009.

Marra, M. (2013). English in the workplace. In B. Paltridge and S. Starfield (Eds.), *The Handbook of English for Specific Purposes* (pp. 175–192). John Wiley and Sons. https://doi.org/10.1002/9781118339855.ch9.

Mason, J. (2002). *Qualitative Researching*. SAGE Publications Ltd.

Mauranen, A., Hynninen, N., & Ranta, E. (2010). English as the academic lingua franca. The ELFA project. *English for Specific Purposes*, *29*(3), 183–190. https://doi.org/10.1016/j.esp.2009.10.001.

Mazzucato, A., & Kic-Drgas, J. (2021). Develop OERs for technology enhanced learning. In P. Limone and R. Di Fuccio (Eds.), *Proceedings of the Second Workshop on Technology Enhanced Learning Environments for Blended Education – The Italian E-Learning Conference*. University of Foggia. http://ceur-ws.org/Vol-3025/.

Medrea, N., & Rus, D. (2012). Challenges in ESP teaching: teaching resources and students' needs. *Procedia Economics and Finance*, *3*, 1165–1169.

Meihami, H., & Werbińska, D. (2022). Role of action research in ESP teachers' professional identity development. *Journal of Research in Applied Linguistics*, *13*(1), 31–43. https://doi.org/10.22055/RALS.2022.17423.

References

Ministry of Education, Science and Sport of the Republic of Slovenia. (2019). *The Education System in the Republic of Slovenia 2018/2019*. Ministry of Education, Science and Sport of the Republic of Slovenia. https://www.gov.si/assets/ministrstva/MIZS/Dokumenti/ENIC-NARIC-center/The-Education-System-in-the-Republic-of-Slovenia-2018-19.pdf.

Nazari, M. (2020). Language for specific purposes teacher education: a scoping review. *MEXTESOL Journal, 44*(4), 1–13.

Nunan, D. (2010). A task-based approach to materials development. *Advances in Language and Literacy Studies, 1*(2), 135–160. 10.7575/aiac.alls.v.1n.2p.135.

Northern Illinois University Center for Innovative Teaching and Learning. (2012). Formative and summative assessment. In Instructional guide for university faculty and teaching assistants. Retrieved from https://www.niu.edu/citl/resources/guides/instructional-guide.

Knowles M, Swanson R, Holton E. (2011). *The adult learner: The definitive classic in adult education and human resource development*. Elsevier.

Omaggio, A. C. (1986). *Teaching Language in Context. Proficiency-Oriented Instruction*. Heinle & Heinle.

Paltridge, B. (2013). Genre and English for specific purposes. In B. Paltridge and S. Starfield (Eds.), *The Handbook of English for Specific Purposes* (pp. 347–366). John Wiley and Sons. https://doi.org/10.1002/9781118339855.ch18.

Paltridge, B., & Starfield, S. (2013). Introduction. In B. Paltridge and S. Starfield (Eds.), *The Handbook of English for Specific Purposes* (pp. 1–4). John Wiley and Sons. https://doi.org/10.1002/9781118339855.ch.

Pennington, M. C. (2015). Teacher identity in TESOL: A frames perspective. In Y. L. Cheung, S. Ben Said and K. Park (Eds.), *Advances and Current Trends in Language Teacher Identity Research* (pp. 16–30). Routledge.

Petraki, E., & Khat, K. (2020). Challenges and constraints in the design of an ESP course in Cambodia: implications for higher education institutions. *Asia Pacific Journal of Education, 42*(2), 260–275. https://doi.org/10.1080/02188791.2020.1798738.

Podgoršek, S., Jurkovič, V., Dostal, M., & Mertelj, D. (2021). Analiza izobraževalnih potreb visokošolskih učiteljev tujih jezikov stroke v Sloveniji. *Sodobna pedagogika, 72*(3), 94–110.

Przybył, J. (2022). Reflecting on the roles of LSP teachers. In J. Kic-Drgas and J. Woźniak (Eds.), *Perspectives on LSP Teacher Training in Poland* (pp. 134–151). FRSE Publications.

Puppin, L. (2007). A paradigm shift: from paper-and-pencil tests to performance-based assessment. *English Teaching Forum, 45*(4), 10–17.

Razpotnik, B. (2022). *The Share of Tertiary-educated Population Exceeded One Quarter*. Statistical Office of the Republic of Slovenia. https://www.stat.si/StatWeb/en/News/Index/10772.

Richards, J. C. (2001). *Curriculum Development in Language Teaching*. Cambridge University Press.

Richards, K. (1997). Teachers for specific purposes. In R. Howard and G. Brown (Eds.), *Teacher Education for Languages for Specific Purposes* (pp. 115–126). Multilingual Matters.

Robinson, P. (1991). *ESP Today: Practitioner's Guide*. Prentice Hall.

Ronaldo O., & Pamungkas, R. W. S. (2020). The needs for English learning material in mechanical engineering department at Institute Technology of Padang. *Journal of Asian Studies: Culture, Language, Art and Communications, 1*(1), 27–37.

Rossi, P. H., Lipsey, M. W., & Freeman, H. E. (2004). *Evaluation: A Systematic Approach.* Sage Publication.

Rubdy, R. (2003). Selection of materials. In B. Tomlinson (Ed.), *Developing Materials for Language Teaching* (pp. 37–57). Continuum.

Sierocka H. (2013). Developing LSP/ESP materials for legal professionals. In P. Vičič (Ed.), *The Role of Languages for Specific Purposes in Intercultural Communication* (pp. 246–254). University of Maribor.

Skela, J. (2019). A journey through the landscapes of language education. In A. Kostoulas (Ed.), *Challenging Boundaries in Language Education, Second Language Learning and Teaching* (pp. 15–32). Springer. https://doi.org/10.1007/978-3-030-17057-8_2.

Skela, J., & Burazer, L. (2023). *Teacher Development Resource Book for Pre-service ELT Education Programs.* Tangram.

Słocińska A. (2013). Procesy dzielenia się wiedzą jako warunek rozwoju współczesnych organizacji. In A. Czech & A. Szpilt (Eds.), *Nauki o zarządzaniu dla przedsiębiorstw i biznesu* (pp. 65–81). University of Katowice.

Sowa, M. (2015). Specjalizacja nauczycielska na filologii romańskiej a kompetencje nauczyciela języka specjalistycznego. *Linguodidactica, 19,* 240–254.

Sowa, M. (2016). Nauczyciel języka specjalistycznego: pomiędzy standardami kształcenia a rzeczywistością zawodową. *Języki obce w szkole, 4,* 12–17.

Sowa, M. (2022a). Potrzeby nauczycieli języków obcych specjalistycznych względem przygotowania i realizacji procesu dydaktycznego. Próba diagnozy. In J. Kic-Drgas and J. Woźniak (Eds.), *Perspektywy kształcenia nauczycieli języków specjalistycznych w Polsce* (pp. 30–54). Fundacja Rozwoju Systemu Edukacji.

Sowa, M. (2022b). The needs of LSP teachers in the preparation and implementation of the didactic process. An attempt at diagnosis. In J. Kic-Drgas and J. Woźniak (Eds.), *Perspectives on LSP Teacher Training in Poland* (pp. 28–52). FRSE Publications.

Spencer-Oatey, H., & Franklin, P. (2009). *Intercultural Interaction: A Multidisciplinary Approach to Intercultural Communication.* Springer.

Stewart, T. (2018). Expanding possibilities for ESP practitioners through interdisciplinary team teaching. In Y. Kırkgöz and K. Dikilitaş (Eds.), *Key Issues in English for Specific Purposes in Higher Education* (pp. 141–156). Springer.

Strevens, P. (1977). *New Orientations in the Teaching of English.* Oxford University Press.

Svetlin Kastelic, N. (2017). *By Knowing English, the Most Frequently Spoken Foreign Language in Slovenia, We Are Part of Europe and the World.* Statistical Office of the Republic of Slovenia. https://www.stat.si/StatWeb/en/News/Index/6936.

Szerszeń, P. (2014). Kilka uwag na temat optymalnego czasu rozpoczynania nauki języka specjalistycznego i możliwości jej realizacji. *Lingwistyka Stosowana, 9,* 133–149.

Szymańska-Tworek, A., & Makowska-Songin, J. (2019). Teacher quality as a prerequisite for quality education: needs and expectations of ESP teachers towards professional development in Polish tertiary education context. In D. Gabryś-Barker and R. Kalamarz (Eds.), *Quality in Language Teaching. Theoretical Considerations and Practical Solutions* (pp. 67–99). University of Silesia Press.

Tao, J., & Gao, X. (2018). Identity constructions of ESP teachers in a Chinese university. *English for Specific Purposes, 49*, 1–13. https://doi.org/10.1016/j.esp.2017.09.003.

The Bologna Declaration of 19 June 1999, http://www.ond.vlaanderen.be/hogeronderwijs/bologna/documents/MDC/BOLOGNA_DECLARATION1.pdf.

Thompson, G., & McKinley, J. (2018). Integration of content and language learning. In J. I. Liontas, M. Delli Carpini and S. Abrar-ul-Hassan (Eds.), *The TESOL Encyclopedia of English Language Teaching*. Wiley. https://doi.org/10.1002/9781118784235.eelt0634.

Tomlinson, B. (Ed). (1998). *Materials Development in Language Teaching*. Cambridge University Press.

TRAILS. (2021). *TRAILS E-companion Book*. TRAILS.

Tudor, I. (1997). LSP or language education. In R. Howard and G. Brown (Eds.), *Teacher Education for Languages for Specific Purposes* (pp. 90–102). Multilingual Matters.

Turula, A. & Gajewska, E. (2019). Towards a Common Competence Framework for LSP Teachers. Catapult Consortium. Retrieved August 28, 2021 from http://catapult-project.eu/?smd_process_download=1&download_id=1066.

University of Ljubljana. (2022). *Master Degree – English*. Faculty of Arts. https://anglistika.ff.uni-lj.si/en/2nd-cycle-english-studies.

University of Maribor. (2022). *Učni načrt predmetov*. Faculty of Arts. https://ff.um.si/wp-content/uploads/ucni_nacrti_PA_22_23.pdf.

University of Primorska. (2022). *Didaktika strokovnih jezikov/Didactics of Languages for Specific Purposes*. Faculty of Humanities. https://fhs.upr.si/magistrski-studij/pedagoska-smer/italijanistika/predmetnik/.

Van der Yeught, M. (2016). Developing English for specific purposes (ESP) in Europe: mainstream approaches and complementary advances. *13th ESSE Conference*. National University of Ireland.

Varghese, M., Morgan, B., Johnston, B., & Johnson, K. A. (2005). Theorizing language teacher identity: three perspectives and beyond. *Journal of Language Identity, 4*(1) 21–44. https://doi.org/10.1207/s15327701jlie0401_2.

Vega Umaña, A. L. (2020). On the nature of ESP teachers' expertise: results from a survey about ESP teaching in French higher education. In M. Sowa (Ed.), *In Search of the LSP Teacher's Competencies* (pp. 203–221). Peter Lang.

Vičič, P., Gajšt, N., & Plos, A. (Eds.) (2018). Conference Proceedings/10th International Language Conference on "The Importance of Learning Professional Foreign Languages for Communication between Cultures", 20 and 21 September 2018, Celje, Slovenia. University of Maribor Press. https://press.um.si/index.php/ump/catalog/book/399.

Vos, L. (2013). Improving international marketing programs to reflect global complexity and risk: curriculum drivers and constraints. *Journal of Teaching in International Business, 24*(2), 81–106. https://doi.org/10.1080/08975930.2013.819257.

Wąsikiewicz-Firlej, E., Szczepaniak-Kozak, A., & Lankiewicz, H. (2022). *Doświadczenie pobytu w Polsce w narracjach zagranicznych studentów*. Wydawnictwo FRSE.

Wenger, E. (1998). *Communities of Practice: Learning, Meaning and Identity*. Cambridge University Press.

Woodrow, L. (2018). *Course Design in English for Specific Purposes*. Routledge.

Wu, W. M., & Stansfield, C. W. (2001). Towards authenticity of task in test development. *Language Testing, 18*(2), 187–206. https://doi.org/10.1191/026553201678777077.

Yaza, B., & Lindahl, K. (Eds.) (2020). *Language Teacher Identity in TESOL. Teacher Education and Practice as Identity Work.* Routledge.

Živković, S. (2016). The ESP technology-supported learning environment. *European Journal of Social Sciences Education and Research, 6*(1), 154–162.